Discard

LATINO BIOGRAPHY LIBRARY

Roberto Clemente

Baseball Legend

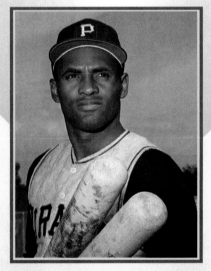

CARIN T. FORD

Enslow Publishers, Inc.

40 Industrial Road   PO Box 38
Box 398   Aldershot
Berkeley Heights, NJ 07922   Hants GU12 6BP
USA   UK

http://www.enslow.com

Library of Congress Cataloging-in-Publication Data

Ford, Carin T.
    Roberto Clemente : baseball legend / Carin T. Ford.
       p. cm. — (Latino biography library)
    Includes bibliographical references and index.
    ISBN 0-7660-2485-7 (hardcover)
    1. Clemente, Roberto, 1934–1972—Juvenile literature. 2. Baseball players—Puerto Rico—Biography—Juvenile literature. I. Title. II. Series.
    GV865.C45F67 2005
    796.357'092—dc22

                                 2004017139

Printed in the United States of America

10 9 8 7 6 5 4 3 2

To Our Readers: We have done our best to make sure all Internet Addresses in this book were active and appropriate when we went to press. However, the author and the publisher have no control over and assume no liability for the material available on those Internet sites or on other Web sites they may link to. Any comments or suggestions can be sent by e-mail to comments@enslow.com or to the address on the back cover.

Every effort has been made to locate all copyright holders of material used in this book. If any errors or omissions have occurred, corrections will be made in future editions of this book.

Illustration Credits: AP/Wide World, pp. 1, 3, 6–7, 8, 13, 17, 24, 26, 30, 37, 39, 46, 48, 51, 52, 56, 59, 64, 70, 76, 78, 82, 90, 95, 99, 103, 108, 110, 114; Carnegie Library of Pittsburgh, pp. 62, 66; Enslow Publishers, Inc., p. 12; Library of Congress, p. 14; National Baseball Hall of Fame Library, Cooperstown, NY, p. 4; Photos.com, p. 20.

Cover Illustration: AP/Wide World

Contents

Major-league talent scouts came to watch Clemente play on the Santurce Cangrejeros (Crabbers).

1

The Dream

Roberto Clemente had dreamed about baseball for most of his nineteen years. As a child, he had thrown rubber balls against his bedroom ceiling hour after hour. When he was too poor to buy a rubber ball, he made balls out of old magazines and newspapers. As long as Roberto had something to throw and something to hit, he was happy. Baseball meant everything to him.

> *"I would lay in bed throwing the ball against the wall."*[1]
> —Clemente

Now, only months away from his twentieth birthday, Roberto was signing a contract with a major league ball club in the United States. He would be leaving his home in Puerto Rico, an island in the West Indies. His dream of a career playing baseball was coming true.

During the off-season in 1954, Willie Mays of the New York Giants played in the Puerto Rican Winter League.

At that time, Puerto Rico was a territory of the United States. The island had been hit hard by the economic depression of the 1930s and 1940s. Most people were poor. Many were facing starvation. Although Roberto's family was luckier than most, there was little money to spare. For Roberto and his friends, broomsticks or the limbs of guava trees had served as baseball bats. The boys crushed tin cans for balls, and when there were no cans available, they used stones and rocks.

Puerto Rican Ballplayers

Before Clemente, only a few Puerto Ricans had made it to the major leagues. In those days, Latino ballplayers faced some of the same prejudices as African Americans. Hiram Gabriel Bithorn pitched for the Chicago Cubs in the early 1940s. Luis Rodríguez Olmo played the outfield for the Brooklyn Dodgers in 1943, then moved on to the Boston Braves. But these players did not become superstars like Clemente.

James "Buster" Clarkson, who managed the Santurce team, said that when Roberto played on the Crabbers, he "had a few rough spots, but he never made the same mistake twice. . . . He listened to what he was told and he did it."[2]

Since his late teens, Roberto had been playing for the Santurce Cangrejeros (Crabbers) in the Puerto Rican Winter League. It was here that he had attracted the attention of some major league scouts. Roberto's outstanding fielding skills drew representatives from the Brooklyn Dodgers, Milwaukee Braves, New York Giants, St. Louis Cardinals, New York Yankees, and other teams. As a result, scouts from nine different teams considered offering Roberto a contract during the winter of 1953.

Roberto's first major league offer came from the Giants organization. The legendary ballplayer Willie Mays

The impressive Dodgers lineup included Jackie Robinson, left, and Roy Campanella, right.

had been playing for the Giants since 1951. An outfield that included Mays and Clemente would be almost too good to be true. Still, the Giants knew that Roberto's hitting was not as strong as his throwing. They were concerned that he would not be a complete player once he reached the major leagues, so their offer was not a very generous one.

The Dodgers' managers, possibly alarmed at the idea of *facing* an outfield that included both Mays and Clemente, were willing to take a chance. They offered Clemente a yearly salary of $5,000, plus a $10,000 signing bonus—an extra sum of money that is paid when the contract is signed. It was a large amount of money for a Latino player at that time. The money interested Clemente, as did the idea of living in New York City, the home to thousands of Puerto Rican immigrants. Roberto told the Dodgers he would sign with them.

When the Braves heard about the Dodgers' offer, they told Clemente they would give him a signing bonus of nearly $30,000.[3] Clemente was not sure what to do. It was tempting. Still, the team did not have the lineup of stars that the Dodgers boasted—players such as Roy Campanella and Jackie Robinson. Also, he did not know much about the city of Milwaukee.

Unsure of what to do, Roberto talked to his parents. There was no uncertainty in the Clementes' minds. Their son had given his word to the Dodgers. A person does not go back on his word, they said.

On February 19, 1954, Roberto co-signed the contract

with his father. Melchor Clemente, who could not read or write, made an X on the document.[4] Roberto Clemente would be playing with the Dodger organization. He would start on their minor league team in Montreal, Canada. Most athletes spend several years in the minor leagues before making it to the major leagues.

Roberto was saying good-bye to poverty, his home, and his family. The dream had become a reality.

Growing Up

Roberto Clemente Walker was born on August 18, 1934, in the San Anton barrio (neighborhood) in Carolina, Puerto Rico. His parents were Luisa Walker and Melchor Clemente. As was the custom in Puerto Rico, Roberto's first name was followed by his father's last name and then his mother's last name. Later, when he lived in the United States, Roberto would use only his father's last name—Clemente.

When Roberto was a little boy, his parents gave him the nickname Momen. As the years passed, no one could remember what it meant.[1] Roberto was the youngest child in the family. The other children were Matino, Andres, Osvaldo, and Ana Iris. His mother also had three children from a previous marriage—Luis, Oquendo, and Rosa Maria.

Roberto's life was not an easy one. Yet he was taught not to be ashamed of the fact that his family was poor.

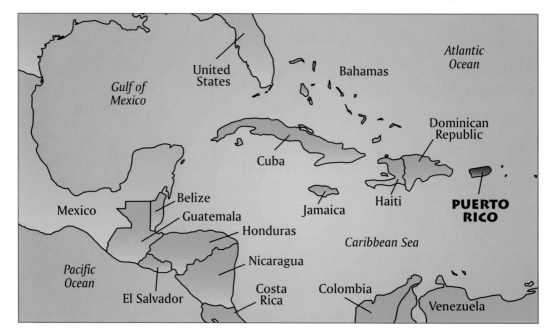

Clemente was born on the island of Puerto Rico.

His parents instilled in him the value of hard work and the importance of always carrying oneself with pride and dignity. Melchor Clemente told Roberto, "I want you to become a good man, a serious man."[2]

Melchor worked as the foreman on a sugarcane plantation. Sugarcane grew well in the hot, tropical climate, where temperatures usually average 82 degrees F. each day. At that time, sugarcane was the chief crop exported from Puerto Rico.

The island was going through hard economic times in the 1930s. Melchor was one of the luckier Puerto Ricans. He earned forty-five cents a day at his job. Back then, the average Puerto Rican was earning about thirty cents a day. To add to his income, Melchor also helped deliver sand and gravel for a local construction company. Even so, there was never enough money with a house full of children to feed.

Luisa Clemente worked as hard as her husband. She woke up at one o'clock each morning to go to her job as a laundress. She also prepared the food that was served to the workers on the sugarcane plantation. Years later, Roberto would remember that his mother had no time or money for leisure activities. She never went out to a movie or a show. She never even learned how to dance.

Roberto's parents always made sure there was enough food for the children. Roberto and his brothers and

Cutting sugarcane stalks by hand is a difficult, dirty job. Sugar is made from the juice of the sugarcane plant.

Roberto and his family lived in a poor neighborhood like this one.

sisters ate first; Melchor and Luisa then ate whatever was left. There was no complaining when the family gathered at the dinner table each night. They were happy to spend time together and did not see themselves as unfortunate. "We would sit down to eat and make jokes and talk and eat whatever there was," Roberto said.[3]

Roberto learned the meaning of hard work early on. When he was nine, he asked his father for a bicycle. The Clementes did not have any money to spare. His father told him he needed to earn the money himself—about $27. So Roberto went to work. Every day at 6 A.M., he carried a neighbor's milk can to the country store, which was located a half mile away. After the can was filled with milk, he lugged it back to the neighbor. It took Roberto three years to earn enough money to buy a secondhand bicycle.

Roberto worked at various other jobs as a boy, including helping his father load the construction trucks. In school Roberto was a good student, though not an outstanding one. He respected his teachers and was quiet and well behaved.

According to his mother, Roberto was always a thoughtful boy. "Even when he was small, if some neighbor died, he went to their house to help out," she said. "When he grew older, he was always the first to offer his shoulder to help carry the coffin."[4]

All Roberto's spare time was devoted to baseball. When he was not playing in a neighborhood game, he was throwing a pink rubber ball against the walls and ceilings of his house. When he was not throwing the pink ball, he was squeezing it to strengthen the muscles in his arms. "I would be lost without baseball," Roberto said many years later. "I don't think I could stand being away from it as long as I was alive."[6]

Roberto joined his first neighborhood team when he was eight. Many of the boys he played against were

> *"When I was a boy, I realized what lovely persons my father and mother were."*[5]
>
> —Clemente

15

"I wanted to have work, to be a good man. I grew up with that on my mind."[7]

—Clemente

older. Still, young Roberto did well with his bat made from a guava tree branch, a glove made from a coffee bean sack, and a ball formed from knotted rags.

He played all day, missing meals and continuing the game until it was too dark to see. Although it was clearly Roberto's dream to become a baseball player, his mother hoped he would become an engineer. In desperation one day, she took his bat and tried to burn it, but Roberto pulled it out of the fire. In later years, Luisa Clemente remembered that incident and said she had been wrong to try to turn her son away from baseball.

Roberto's parents were very strict, but he adored them. Once, Melchor Clemente became sick and had to be hospitalized. Roberto was very young and hospital rules would not let him visit. But that did not stop Roberto. He climbed a palm tree and sneaked into his father's room through the window.

When Roberto was fourteen, he was playing sandlot ball one day with his friends. Roberto Marín stopped to watch the game. Marín, a part-time high school teacher, also traveled throughout Puerto Rico as a rice salesman for the Sello Rojo rice company. Sello Rojo sponsored one of the slow-pitch softball teams in San Juan, Puerto

Give a kid a stick—like this youngster in Cuba—and you have the makings of a ballgame. Roberto and his friends used tree branches and broomsticks as bats.

Rico. Marín helped organize the team, and he also scouted talented players.

That day, as usual, Roberto and the other boys were playing with their broomsticks and empty tomato sauce cans. Marín spotted one boy who seemed to have extraordinary athletic ability. That boy was Roberto Clemente.

Roberto was recruited to play

"I would be lost without baseball."[8]

—Clemente

shortstop on the Sello Rojo softball team. For the first time, he would be wearing a team uniform. He was not a strong hitter and he batted near the bottom of the lineup—but his fielding was exceptional. Onlookers enjoyed watching the cap fly off Roberto's head as he made spectacular plays.

Roberto did so well that he was chosen to take part in a special competition called Future Stars. Being selected for this was a great honor for Roberto, especially considering that most of the other players were two years older than he was.

"I see this one kid . . . he never strike out. Bam! Bam! Bam! Tin cans all over the field. I say, 'Who are you?' "[9]

—*Roberto Marín*

After watching Roberto for two seasons, Marín decided to move him to the outfield, where Roberto stayed for the rest of his career. His powerful throwing arm made him a natural at the position.

Roberto's strength also made him outstanding at throwing the javelin, a light spear used in track events. Besides making the district all-star baseball team three years in a row, Roberto participated on the track and field team at Julio Vizcarrondo High School. He threw the javelin, ran the 400 meters, and competed in the high jump and the triple jump (where the athlete takes a running start and performs a series of leaps). While Roberto could high-jump 6 feet and triple-jump 45 feet, the javelin was where he really excelled, throwing up to 190 feet. When he was in his junior year, many people wondered whether Roberto would be throwing the javelin in the 1952 Olympic Games to be held in Helsinki, Finland. By that time, though, his interests already lay elsewhere.

In high school Roberto showed leadership qualities and an interest in helping others. When his teacher told the class one day that the schoolyard was full of weeds and that the cleanup would be expensive, Roberto offered to help. He volunteered the services of his class-mates, too.

While he was still in high school, Roberto decided he wanted a career in baseball. He had recently joined an AA league baseball team—the equal of a team in the minor leagues—owned by Ferdinand Juncos and man-aged by Monchile Concepción. Now focusing on his baseball skills, Roberto began to show improvement in his hitting. Marín believed Roberto played better than

The Lure of the Game

When Roberto visited San Juan to buy lottery tickets for his father, he liked to stop off at Sixto Escobar Stadium and watch the ballgame that was being played there. One time, a foul ball was hit out of the park. Roberto kept the ball and slept with it.

Javelin-throwing calls for a powerful throwing arm. It was no surprise that Roberto, who excelled at the javelin, was an amazing outfielder.

many of the professionals who took part in Puerto Rico's winter league. He was so impressed that he contacted Pedrín Zorrilla, a scout for the Brooklyn Dodgers.

According to Marín, as soon as Zorrilla looked at Roberto, he commented, "*Caramba* [my goodness], what a pair of hands!"

Marín replied, "He's an unpolished gem."[10]

Shortly after meeting Roberto, Zorrilla went to see him in a baseball game. Roberto played well. He had a solid hit, made two catches in center field, and threw out a runner who was trying to score at home plate.

Zorrilla was also the owner of the Santurce Crabbers, a team in the Puerto Rican Winter League. A tryout camp was held one day at the Sixto Escobar Stadium. It was sponsored by Zorrilla's Crabbers as well as the Dodgers. Through the years, the majority of young men showing up at tryout camp had little talent. But that day, the camp included seventeen-year-old Roberto, wearing a T-shirt and wrinkled baseball pants.

Roberto was asked first to throw from the outfield. Standing in center field, Roberto threw balls that seemed to fly like bullets; his accuracy was dead-on. When Alex "Al" Campanis, the head scout in the Caribbean for the Dodgers, saw one spectacular throw, he could not believe his eyes. He asked Roberto to do it again—and Roberto did.

The young athletes were then asked to run the sixty-yard dash. Roberto was clocked at 6.4 seconds. Campanis looked at his stopwatch in disbelief. The world record was only three-tenths of a second faster. He asked Roberto to run it again. Roberto did—in exactly the same time.

All that remained to be seen was whether or not Roberto could hit. The other seventy-one players were sent home, and Roberto was given a bat. His swinging style was undisciplined: He stood far away from the plate, both feet

> **Roberto threw balls that seemed to fly like bullets; his accuracy was dead-on.**

coming off the ground. Yet he continued to rip line drives to right field, center field, and some to left field. Roberto hit at least ten balls over the fence.

Years later, Campanis would say of Roberto, "He was the greatest natural athlete I have ever seen as a free agent."[11] A free agent is someone who is not bound by a contract to any team.

Since Roberto was only seventeen, he could not sign a major league baseball contract. He would have to wait another year. Instead he signed on with Zorrilla's Santurce team for $40 to $45 a week plus a bonus of $400. Roberto's father asked a neighbor to read through the contract. Then Melchor Clemente signed the paper with an X on October 9, 1952.

It was Roberto's first contract as a professional baseball player.

3

The Minor Leagues

The Santurce Crabbers were a powerful team in the Puerto Rican Winter League. Their season lasted approximately four months and included seventy-two games in all, an average of about four games each week. The winter league included some African-American baseball stars. At that time, many of these athletes played in the Negro Leagues during the regular baseball season.

The Negro Leagues had existed since 1868. In the 1880s and 1890s, a few African Americans were permitted to play on white teams. Then, as the 1800s drew to a close, blacks were barred from the major leagues. Even though the top African-American players were every bit as good as the top white players, black athletes were no longer allowed to play alongside whites.

The Negro Leagues boasted many outstanding athletes, some of whom were paid more than the white players in the National and American Leagues. There was Leroy "Satchel" Paige, Andrew "Rube" Foster, and Monte Irvin—Roberto's hero as a young boy. Six out of the first seven rookies of the year for the National League in major league baseball were men who had gotten their start in the Negro Leagues.[1] Jackie Robinson, Don Newcombe, and Willie Mays all played in the Negro Leagues before they were allowed to join the major leagues. "We had good lives," said Buck O'Neil, a Negro League star who went on to become the first black coach ever hired by a major league team. "This was the third largest black business in America. We rode on good buses. . . . The money we made wasn't bad, either."[2]

One of the top Negro League teams was the St. Paul Gophers, shown here in 1909.

When Jackie Robinson joined the Brooklyn Dodgers in 1947, he broke the color barrier in major league baseball and opened the door for other black players. It was a difficult road for Robinson. Ordered not to fight back—verbally or physically—he had to put up with racial insults and petitions drawn up by players who wanted to remove him from the Dodgers as well as the National League. He also had to deal with physical and emotional abuse, hate mail, and death threats to himself and his family. But the six-time All-Star athlete, who also won the first Rookie of the Year award, was determined to see it through. "I will not forget that I am representative of a whole race of people who are pulling for me," Robinson said.[3]

Robinson paved the way for integration in major league baseball—and with that integration came the end of the Negro Leagues. By 1953, there were only four teams left in the Negro Leagues and twenty African Americans playing on seven major league ball clubs.[4] These players included Willie Mays, Henry "Hank" Aaron, and Ernie Banks.

The Negro Leagues

While major league teams played only in large cities, the Negro Leagues appeared wherever there was a ballfield. They played on farms, in prisons, just about anywhere. The Negro League games drew large crowds of thirty-five thousand to forty thousand, about the same number of spectators as major league games.

Jackie Robinson, above, the first African American in the major leagues, opened the door for players like Roberto Clemente.

The Crabbers, the best team in the Puerto Rican Winter League, had many top black baseball stars in its lineup. Because Clemente was a newcomer to the league, he spent most of his first season on the bench. Zorrilla was a cautious man. He did not want to put an inexperienced player on the field; he also worried that the veterans on the team would resent the young outfielder. Clemente was very unhappy about the situation. "You've got to talk to the manager, because if he doesn't play me I'm quitting," he told Marín at one point.[5]

Clemente got a break when the Crabbers loaded the bases during one game. The player coming up was Bob Thurman, an African American who would go on to join the major leagues in 1955. Thurman was an excellent hitter except when he faced a left-handed pitcher. The other team, the Caguas, had a lefty on the mound, so Clemente was asked to go in for Thurman. He smacked a double into right field that won the game for the Crabbers. After that game, Clemente did not spend as much time on the bench. Still, by the end of the season, after seventy-seven times at bat in seventy games, his batting average was a mediocre .234.

Clemente's experience in the Puerto Rican Winter

> *Robinson had to put up with insults and abuse, but he would not quit.*

League taught him a lot. An erratic hitter at that time, Clemente tended to drag his front foot toward third base rather than step toward the pitcher as he swung the bat. To correct this habit, his manager, Buster Clarkson, placed a bat behind Clemente's left foot during batting practice. Clemente worked hard to change his stride, and Clarkson was impressed with the young athlete's desire to improve.

During his second season, Clemente also learned from his teammate Willie Mays. Outfielder Mays had debuted in the major leagues in 1951 and was already a star. He played center field in the winter leagues while Clemente played left field. Five years older than Clemente, Mays showed the younger player such things as how outfielders back each other up when fielding a ball. Clemente improved, and during that second season (1953–1954), he was put into the starting lineup. Although some of the veteran ballplayers were not happy about this change, Clarkson felt that Clemente was too good to leave on the bench. Clarkson's instincts paid off as Clemente's batting average rose to .288 that year.[7]

"If he doesn't play me I'm quitting."[6]
—Clemente

Clemente had signed with the Dodger organization in 1954, leaving Puerto Rico after the winter league season. The minor league team in Montreal was one of three Canadian teams in the International League; the

Willie Mays

Willie Mays was one of baseball's greatest players. When he was sixteen years old, he joined the Birmingham Black Barons, a Negro League team. At first, Mays's father allowed him to play only home games, because he did not want his teenaged son missing school. When Mays graduated high school, he signed with the New York Giants. He quickly became known as an amazing fielder as well as a home run hitter. Over the course of his twenty-two-year career, he hit 3,283 hits and 660 home runs, which put him fourth among the major league home run hitters.

other two were Ottawa and Toronto. There was also a club in Havana, Cuba, along with four United States teams, located in Richmond, Virginia, and the New York cities of Buffalo, Rochester, and Syracuse.

The joy of signing with a major league organization quickly evaporated as Clemente was faced with a new experience: dealing with prejudice because of the color of his skin. The Montreal team occasionally traveled south to Richmond, Virginia. This was before the civil rights progress in the 1960s, and most public places in the South, including the restaurants and hotels, were segregated—meaning blacks and whites had separate facilities. Everything from public transportation to schools to water fountains was segregated. Often, African Americans were forbidden to participate in activities involving whites.

For the first time in his life, Clemente was told he could not eat in the same restaurants or stay in the same hotels as white people. He discovered that the Montreal team was unofficially split into two groups on the basis of the players' skin color. Clemente found himself in the same situation as his black teammates Sandy Amoros, Joe Black, and Chico Fernandez.

The black players from the United States had been treated like second-class citizens all their lives. For the Puerto Rican–born Clemente, however, it was a disturbing new experience.

Legalized segregation in the South was a shock to the Puerto Rican native Roberto Clemente.

Pitcher Joe Black, born in Plainfield, New Jersey, had begun his career in the Negro Leagues before joining the Dodgers in the early 1950s. In his travels to Latin American countries, he had seen little, if any, segregation. Occasionally, he noted, lighter-skinned citizens would receive better treatment than those with darker skin. Black observed that it was difficult for many Latino players to adjust to life in the United States, where they were suddenly confronted with racial boundaries.[8]

This was the situation in which Clemente found himself. He experienced far less prejudice when the Royals played at home in Montreal, though there was an incident in Canada where Clemente was told he could not talk to a white woman. Still, for the most part, blacks could go anywhere in Montreal without being confronted with prejudice.

Another problem for Clemente in his new ball club was his difficulty in speaking and understanding English. He had studied English in high school, but he had never before needed to communicate in a language other than Spanish. When he was cursed on the field one day by a player from the opposing team, Clemente thanked the man. He thought he had been given a compliment.

Clemente's biggest problem, though, was that he was spending most of his time on the bench. It seemed as if the better he played, the more time he sat out. On the other hand, when he came to the plate and struck out, he remained in the lineup. What was going on?

The Dodgers were using a strategy to protect their investment. The rules in baseball at that time allowed other teams to draft any player who received a bonus and salary of more than $4,000 and was not on the major league roster for the entire season. Clemente fit these criteria.

> **Why was Clemente spending so much time on the bench instead of out in the field?**

He was not playing for the Dodgers major league club in Brooklyn. Instead he was on their minor league team in Montreal. With a bonus and salary totaling $15,000, he was eligible to be picked up by another ball club. Hoping to prevent this from happening, his team in Montreal gave him very little playing time. If Clemente did not get to show off his ability, the managers reasoned, no one would take any interest in drafting him. The Dodgers did not want to lose Clemente.

For Clemente, this treatment was devastating. His lifelong dream of signing with a major league ball club had come true, yet he was not being allowed to play. During one of the final games of the season, Clemente's patience ran out. The manager put in a pinch-hitter— that is, another player was taking Clemente's place in the batting lineup. Clemente stormed out of the ballpark in disgust. He intended to pack up his belongings, leave the Royals, and return to Puerto Rico.

Howie Haak, a scout for the Pittsburgh Pirates, had been sent to Montreal to take a look at Clemente. He showed up at the ballpark too late. Hurrying over to Clemente's hotel, Haak rapped on the door until Clemente answered. Leaving the team would put Clemente on the suspended list, said Haak. It would then be impossible for any other team to draft him— and the Pirates were definitely interested in drafting Clemente.[9]

Soon after, Clemente spoke with Al Campanis, the scout who had first seen him in Escobar Stadium several years earlier. Campanis, too, urged Clemente to be patient. He assured the frustrated ballplayer that everything would work out.

The Pittsburgh Pirates had first pick in the National League draft that year. They were considering drafting the Montreal pitcher Joe Black. Then Pittsburgh's scout traveled to Richmond, Virginia, to see the Montreal team play. Clemente's powerful throwing arm and unusual but effective batting style caught the scout's eye. When the major league clubs met in New York City on November 22, 1954, the last-place Pirates announced their first choice in the draft: Roberto Clemente.

4

The Pirates

Clemente was in Puerto Rico for the off-season—the time of year when major league baseball is not being played—when he heard he had been drafted to the Pirates.

Most of Clemente's attention at the time was focused on his older brother, Luis, who had been diagnosed with a brain tumor. Roberto wanted to spend as much time as possible with Luis. Driving home from one of his final trips to the hospital before his brother died, Roberto was hit by a drunk driver who had raced through a red light at sixty miles per hour. Three of Clemente's spinal discs were jarred loose in the crash. Back pain would plague him for the rest of his baseball career.

> **"I didn't even know where Pittsburgh was."[1]**
>
> **—Clemente**

Clemente did not have much time to recover before the Pirates' spring training began in Fort Myers, Florida. During a preseason game, Clemente once again became the victim of the prejudice of the American South. The Pirates were scheduled to play an exhibition game against the Baltimore Orioles in Birmingham, Alabama. The officials in Birmingham had recently passed a ruling that forbade blacks and whites to participate in sporting events together. Clemente and two other players were told not to put on their uniforms for the game. They would not be allowed to play.[2]

In spite of the problems of racism and Clemente's continuing difficulty in speaking English, he did well during spring training. However, he did not win a spot in the starting lineup when the regular season began. Roman Mejias of Cuba landed the right-field position. Tom Saffell played center field, and Frank Thomas, a Pirates veteran, took left field. For the first few games of the season, Clemente sat on the bench.

> "Not to speak the language meant you were different."[3]
>
> —Clemente

The Pirates home games were played at Forbes Field. Home to the Pirates since 1909, the stadium was named after British general John Forbes, who captured Fort Pitt from the French during the French and Indian War in 1758. The park was huge, housing about thirty-five thousand spectators. From home plate to the left-field wall was 365 feet—the longest distance in the National League—making Forbes one of the hardest parks in which to hit a home run. The other dimensions were 406 feet for left center field, 435 for center, 408 for right center, and 300 for right field.[4] "When I first saw Forbes Field, I said, 'Forget home runs,'" said Clemente. "I was strong, but nobody was that strong. I became a line-drive hitter."[5]

Although the Pirates had captured three straight championships in 1901, 1902, and 1903, by the time Clemente began playing with the Pirates in 1955 the team seemed to be stuck at the bottom of the league. In four of the last five years, they had finished dead last. The other year, they came in next to last. The Pirates had not captured the league title since 1927, and the last time they had won the World Series was in 1925.

When Clemente took his first major league at-bat, he wore the number 21 on his uniform. He had decided on the number one day when he was sitting in a movie theater. He wrote out his full name, Roberto Clemente Walker, on a scrap of paper and counted the letters. There were twenty-one.

Clemente's first at-bat took place on April 17, 1955. He faced Brooklyn Dodgers' left hander Johnny Podres, who had won eleven games the previous year. Third in the order, Clemente stepped up to the plate with two outs. He hit the ball to the left side of the infield and made it safely to first base. He then scored on a triple

When Clemente joined the Pittsburgh Pirates in 1955, they were at the bottom of the league. He was eager to help improve the team's standing.

by Frank Thomas, putting the Pirates temporarily ahead of the Dodgers. They would eventually lose the game 10–3.

Clemente had played well, and he found himself starting again in the second game of that day's double-header. Playing center field (he had played right in the first game), he hit a single and a double. However, the Dodgers won again, 3–2.

On April 18, Clemente stayed in the lineup against the New York Giants, starting in right field. Not only did he throw out a runner and get a hit, he also slugged an inside-the-park home run. Still, the Pirates lost, 12–3.

Clemente totaled nine hits during his first week of regular play. Continuing to swing freely, he went after any pitch that was in the general area of the strike zone. When he struck out, he would angrily throw his plastic helmet to the ground. He said he cracked twenty-two helmets during his first season and had to pay the Pirates a total of $220 for damaging the equipment. It was a lot of money for Clemente, so he learned to control his outbreaks.

As his rookie season progressed, Clemente's hitting started to take a downward turn. He swung at anything. Pitchers discovered that he was an easy target for off-speed pitches. Clemente hated walking and averaged only one walk for every eighteen times at bat. He struck out one out of every eight times he came up to the plate.

The superstar Willie Mays gave Clemente some good advice. Mays advised him to act "mean" when he

Clemente, left, was often compared to superstar Willie Mays, right.

was at the plate.[6] He told Clemente that pitchers would try to knock him down, but he had to act as if nothing bothered him. Mays was right: The pitchers were trying to fluster the young ballplayer. Nelson Briles was pitching for the St. Louis Cardinals when he faced Clemente. "He would stand all the way in the back of the box and away from the plate," Briles said. "It looked like you had all this room. I pitched him inside . . . and inside *hard*. I knocked him down a couple of times."[7]

Rubén Gomez, who pitched for the New York Giants in the 1950s, later described Clemente as an outstanding athlete who was able to make up for the fact that his batting style was not correct. Like Briles, Gomez believed the only way to get Clemente out was to knock him down with pitches that came close to his body.

"If you didn't, he'd murder you," Gomez said.[8]

That season, Clemente's fielding produced some extraordinary moments. In a May 4 game against the Milwaukee Braves, Clemente bobbled a ball and allowed players to reach second and third. He soon made up for the mistake.

The Pirates were leading 5–4, when Milwaukee's George Crowe came up to the plate. It was the ninth inning with two outs. Crowe blasted a shot to right field that seemed destined to go over the fence for a three-run home run. However, Clemente ran back and stood by the right-field bleachers. Jumping high in the air with his glove reaching over the fence and into the stands, he caught the ball. The Pirates were able to hang on to their lead and win the game.

Clemente was popular from the start with most Pittsburgh fans. He would often sign autographs up to three hours after home games. Some fans even brought sandwiches for Clemente to eat between the games of a double header.

Yet throughout his career, Clemente would be criticized by some teammates, sports writers, and baseball fans for complaining about his injuries. Clemente had been living with back pain ever since the car accident in Puerto Rico. At times it was so excruciating that he was unable to play. Even so, some people expected him to tough it out. Athletes were often told that the key was playing through the pain.

According to Nelson King, who pitched for the Pirates that year, Clemente viewed his body in the same way that a mechanic would look at a racing car. He devoted a lot of time to keeping it in excellent shape and was concerned when it was not working perfectly. He did not believe in ignoring injuries. Because of this attitude, some players and sportswriters made fun of Clemente, and he was deeply hurt by it, King said.[9]

Clemente had made friends with Roman Mejias, another Latin American Pirates outfielder, and Phil Dorsey, an African-American postal worker whom he met through Pirates pitcher Bob Friend. Dorsey helped Clemente in a variety of ways. He drove him places, handled some of his correspondence, and showed the ballplayer around Pittsburgh. Dorsey also helped Clemente with a troublesome problem. Clemente suffered from insomnia, the inability to get enough sleep. The slightest noise kept him from falling asleep or woke him up. Dorsey found a private home, in a quiet neighborhood, where Clemente could stay.

Sometimes Clemente signed autographs for three hours after a game.

Although he had the highest batting average on the team by June, Clemente finished the season hitting .255. He hit only 5 home runs and 47 RBIs (runs batted in). Out of his 121 hits, 39 had been either doubles or triples. As a team, the Pirates showed little improvement over past years—they finished in last place. Clemente's rookie year had not been an easy one. Along with others in the Pirates' organization, Clemente questioned whether perhaps he had been brought up to the major leagues too quickly.[10]

The issue of prejudice remained a problem. Some players on the Pirates disliked him simply because of the color of his skin. Clemente would always have difficulty understanding prejudice. "I don't believe in color; I believe in people," he said. "I didn't even know about this stuff when I got here."[11]

> **"I don't believe in color; I believe in people."[12]**
>
> **—Clemente**

Some African-American players told Clemente not to say anything about how he was treated. The country had been like this for two hundred years, and Clemente would not be able to change anything, they said. Yet it infuriated Clemente when he heard players on opposing teams shouting out racial slurs at himself, Roman Mejias, or second baseman Curt Roberts, the first African American to play for the Pirates. Clemente also received some hate mail, telling him to go back to Puerto Rico.

The situation was not helped by the way newspaper reporters often wrote about Latin American players. Clemente could speak English, but like most people who learn a new language as an adult, his grammar and word pronunciation were flawed. When sportswriters interviewed Clemente, they usually wrote down his words just as they sounded. For example, Clemente was once quoted in the *Pittsburgh Press* as saying, "I no play so gut yet. Me like hot weather, veree hot. I no run fast cold weather."[13]

These quotes made Clemente and other Spanish-speaking ballplayers sound as if they were not very bright. According to the pitcher Nelson King, American sportswriters were simply not used to talking to Latino players. Like many others, King believed the writers should have corrected the players' grammar and not written down the words exactly as the athletes pro-nounced them.[14]

Language was occasionally a problem on the field as well. During one spring training game against the Baltimore Orioles, Clemente and Roman Mejias were told to hold up on a base, rather than continue running for the next base. Both players ran and were called out, costing the Pirates some runs. However, when manager Fred Haney approached the two men after the game, he realized they had not understood his instructions. After that, Haney bought a Spanish diction-ary to help him communicate with his Latino players.[15]

> "I was lonely."[16]
>
> —Clemente

For the most part, the Pirates' ballplayers did very little to help rookies such as Clemente. There were several older players on the team who may have been worried about losing their positions to the younger athletes. Another reason was that many white players simply did not want to mix with black and Latino players.

The major league baseball season generally runs from April through September. At the end of each season, Clemente returned to Puerto Rico. In addition to playing Winter League ball, he enjoyed working with his hands during his time off. Clemente made ceramic lamps and punch bowls and sewed curtains. He also liked searching the beach for interesting pieces of driftwood that he could paint and polish. Many of these creations decorated his home. Others were given to friends as gifts.

5

Adjusting

Clemente's back continued to trouble him at the start of the 1956 season. In fact, as he approached the age of twenty-two, Clemente decided to give his baseball career one more year. If he was still suffering as much pain, he would quit.

Several changes were made in the Pirates' organization that year. Branch Rickey, who had been president of the club, retired. Joe L. Brown, who took over, started off with a major trade. In exchange for the outfielder Bobby Del Greco, the Pirates received Bill Virdon, an outfielder from the St. Louis Cardinals. Virdon had been Rookie of the Year in 1955.

The club also had a new manager, Bobby Bragan. In the first game on opening day, Clemente learned that Bragan had a very different management style from the quiet Fred Haney. At one point in the game, Bragan wanted to set up a squeeze play. A squeeze play is often

The Pirates called on Baseball Hall of Famer George Sisler to help Clemente improve his batting technique.

called for when a runner is at third base. The batter bunts the ball toward first. While he is getting thrown out running to first base, the runner on third is able to score. When Clemente came up to bat, there was a man on third and one out. Although Bragan had called for a squeeze play, Clemente swung at the ball and fouled it off. Bragan made it clear that he would not put up with similar mistakes: He fined Clemente $25.

Clemente's weak spot was still his hitting. Throughout his career, Clemente always stood far back from the plate. Waiting almost until the last moment, he would swing at the ball with his hands close to his chest. He would reach back so far with his bat, it looked as if he was trying to swat the ball out of the catcher's glove.[1]

The Pirates enlisted the help of George Sisler, a first baseman who was in the Baseball Hall of Fame, to work with Clemente. Sisler noted that Clemente swung at just about any pitch and also bobbed his head constantly when he was at the plate. When he got Clemente to hold his head still, the results came quickly. By mid-June, Clemente was hitting .357, placing him third in the National League.

As Clemente was improving, so was the team. Management had replaced some of the veteran ballplayers and now had a young club, with such players as Bill Mazeroski, Dick Groat, Bob Skinner, Bob Friend, Vernon Law, and, of course, Clemente. Although it would not last, the Pirates found themselves in first place that June.

Former Pirates' president Branch Rickey, center, stops for a word with pitcher Bob Friend, left, and infielder Dick Groat. The wave of young players like Friend, Groat, and Clemente gave the Pirates hope of a winning season.

By the end of the 1956 season, the Pittsburgh ball club had dropped to seventh place. Still, they were only a game behind the New York Giants, who had secured the sixth-place slot. As for Clemente, he had managed to end his second season hitting .311. He had dealt with back pain—along with several other injuries—yet he missed playing in only 7 of the 154 games.

It was an encouraging year for Clemente. He made a number of spectacular plays, and his hitting improved as well. He was also feeling more at home in Pittsburgh.

He spoke English more fluently and had become friendly with some more of his teammates, particularly first baseman Dale Long.

Clemente continued to have difficulties with the press. If he complained about his back or another injury, reporters speculated that he was trying to avoid playing. In addition, cultural differences between Puerto Rico and the United States sometimes led to unfair criticism. In Puerto Rico, a person was expected to accept a compliment and agree with it. In the United States, however, a person was supposed to be modest and usually denied the compliment. Once, when Clemente was told that he was the best defensive right fielder in the game, he agreed. He said he worked hard in order to become the best. To Americans, Clemente's response seemed conceited. For these reasons, his relationship with journalists was often rocky.[2]

Clemente's fans, on the other hand, adored him. They crowded around asking for autographs, easing Clemente's lonely times and making him feel wanted. In later years, as Clemente's fame grew, his fans would bring him cakes on his birthday. The fan mail poured in, too, and Clemente would write back.

Because Clemente had performed well in 1956, he was given a raise in salary that winter. He traveled to Puerto Rico for the off-season and played in the Winter League, hitting .396. Clemente used some of his salary to buy his parents a nice home in the suburbs. Although it cost $12,500, which was a lot of money in Puerto Rico in the mid-1950s, Clemente did not view the house as a big gift.

For the 1957 season, Clemente was once again plagued by back problems. He visited a variety of doctors, looking for relief. One doctor advised him to have his tonsils removed. He did, but the pain continued. He wound up hitting .253 for the year, driving in 30 runs and playing in only 111 out of the 154 games. It would be the worst year in his career.

> *"I am trying to pay [my parents] back for giving me so much."*[3]
>
> —Clemente

Clemente's difficulty in getting enough rest also persisted. The heavy travel schedule during the baseball season and the constant change of hotel rooms was hard for him. To help, the Pirates' management assigned Clemente to a private room without a roommate.

Meanwhile, Bragan had been replaced halfway through the season. The new manager, Danny Murtaugh, had played the infield for the Pirates in the past. Murtaugh was a more daring manager than Bragan, so the Pirates' 1958 season began with an air of excitement. Murtaugh was a determined man who worked his ballplayers hard. The results were apparent from the beginning, with Clemente's batting average soaring to nearly .400.

"I was born to play baseball," said Clemente.

Danny Murtaugh managed the Pirates for many of the years between 1958 and 1973.

For the first time in longer than anyone could remember, the Pittsburgh Pirates were a team to watch. Playing hard in a tight pennant race against the San Francisco Giants and the Milwaukee Braves, the Pirates ended the season in second place.

Although Clemente hit .289 for the year, he had suffered a painful injury in April while making a snap throw from the outfield against the Dodgers. Clemente said he heard his arm crack, and he developed a bone chip in his right elbow. For the next few years, Clemente would throw hard only when he felt he had to.[4] The arm injury as well as his recurring back troubles caused problems between Clemente and Murtaugh. Murtaugh questioned the severity of Clemente's injuries, and in any case, he held the point of view that athletes should play through pain.

After the 1958 season, Clemente spent six months serving at the Marine Corps Recruit Depot in Parris Island, near Beaufort, South Carolina. He showed up at boot camp on October 4, 1958. Not only was Clemente able to give his back a break from baseball, but the drills, hikes, and exercises he was required to do on a daily basis seemed to improve his back. From Parris Island, Clemente went on to Camp LeJeune, North Carolina. This was where the Marines received advanced infantry training. The six months in the Marines caused Clemente to miss spring training.

Pittsburgh fans had high hopes that the 1959 season would be the year their team would finally win the National League championship. But they would have to wait a little longer. The 1950s would end better than they had begun for Pittsburgh, but with no signs of greatness. The team finished in fourth place in 1959, with Clemente hitting .296 after playing in only 105 games. He had been injured again early in the season when a pitch hit him on his right elbow. After forty days on the disabled list, Clemente returned to the lineup in the first week of July. From then till the end of the season, he missed playing in only two games.

Meanwhile, his teammates had also suffered various injuries. So the fans did the only thing they could do— they waited.

6

World Champions

In 1960 Clemente finally seemed to hit his stride. During an early May game in Candlestick Park in San Francisco, Clemente blasted a ball directly into heavy winds for a 450-foot home run. After twenty-seven games, he was batting .336 and won the baseball journalists' "Player of the Month" title for the National League.

At a ceremony on the field the following month, Clemente was given an engraved desk set presented by Harold "Pie" Traynor, a Hall of Famer who played third base for the Pirates in the 1920s and 1930s and managed the team from 1934 to 1939. "He can hit, run, field and throw," said Traynor. "You won't find many with all of those qualifications. Some have two or three, but not many have all four."[1]

Clemente was enjoying himself that season. Like many athletes, he latched on to various superstitions.

When a Dixieland band followed the team to a game on the road and the Pirates lost, Clemente suggested that the musical group brought bad luck and should be kept away. If the Pirates were on a winning streak, Clemente would not change his shirt. Even after winning eleven straight games in 1960, Clemente refused to change his shirt until the Pirates lost.

The team was on a roll, and the players could sense the excitement. "It seemed like from Day One everything happened right," said center fielder Bill Virdon. "Any time we needed a run, any time we needed an out, any time we needed something to happen to win, it happened. Somebody was on our side."[2]

Clemente's average rose to .360 in June, although it fell to .346 during a one-week slump. He continued making exceptional plays in the field as the summer wore on. In early August, the Pirates found themselves leading the San Francisco Giants 1–0 in the seventh inning during a game at Forbes Field. Willie Mays came to bat for the Giants and hit a powerful line drive deep into right field. Clemente ran as fast as he could toward the ball and lunged headfirst into the concrete wall in right field.

> *"He can hit, run, field and throw. You won't find many with all of those qualifications."[3]*
>
> *—Harold "Pie" Traynor*

The crowds went wild for Clemente's daring plays.

Falling to the ground, Clemente lifted his glove after a few seconds—he had made the catch. The Pirates held on to win the game. Meanwhile, Clemente was rushed by ambulance to the hospital, where he received stitches in his chin and was told not to play for a week.

When he was back in the lineup—the stitches still in his chin—Clemente was almost solely responsible for a win against St. Louis. He knocked in all four runs in the 4–1 victory over the Cardinals.

On September 25, 1960, the Pirates found themselves facing the Milwaukee Braves in an away game. For the Pirates to claim the National League title, one of two things had to happen: Either the Pirates had to beat the Braves, or the St. Louis Cardinals had to lose to the Chicago Cubs.

As Clemente came up to bat, the Braves' scoreboard lit up with the message that the Cardinals had just lost. That meant the Pirates had won the pennant, so there was great excitement in the Pirates dugout. Clemente asked Dick Stuart, who was in the on-deck circle, what was going on. Clemente heard the news, returned to home plate, and hit a single to center field. Another batter, Hal Smith, hit a double, and the third-base coach signaled to Clemente to stop at third. Clemente ignored the signal, racing around third and sliding home safely. He was eager to join the celebration in the Pirates dugout.[4] The day ended with a Braves win, but it did not matter. With the Cardinals' loss, the Pirates would be making their first trip to the World Series since 1925.

Tens of thousands of fans greeted the Pirates when they returned to Pittsburgh. Not only had the season been successful, it had been dangerously exciting—twenty-one of the Pirates ninety-five wins had come in the ninth inning.

For the twenty-six-year-old Clemente, the season had been his best ever. He batted .314 with 179 hits, 22 of which were doubles and 16 of which were home runs. He had batted in ninety-four runs.

The Pirates would face the Yankees in the World Series. While it had been thirty-five years since Pittsburgh had played in the championship, the Yankees had captured eight World Series titles in the previous thirteen years. They had been the American League champions ten times in ten years.

The series opened on October 5, 1960, in Pittsburgh. Clemente's mother and brother came to the game. In the first inning, Clemente drove in a run by hitting a ground ball into center field. In the fourth inning, he narrowly avoided a disaster. Yogi Berra hit a ball nearly 420 feet into right field, sending both Virdon and Clemente racing after it. The roar of the crowd drowned out both fielders' calls for the ball, and the men collided. Luckily, neither man was injured, and Virdon managed to hold on to the ball.

The Yankees totaled thirteen hits in the first game, but the Pirates were able to score six runs off their eight

Clemente was popular among Pirates fans, young and old.

hits—including Bill Mazeroski's two-run home run—which gave them the 6–4 win.

In game two, the fans at Forbes Field watched the Pirates get crushed by the Yankees. Among New York's nineteen hits were two home runs and five RBIs by Mickey Mantle. The Pirates' thirteen hits—two by Clemente—scored only three runs. The Pirates went through six pitchers on their way to a 16–3 loss.

> *In 1960, the Pirates played their first World Series since 1925.*

Game three took place at Yankee Stadium with an attendance of seventy thousand. The Yankee pitching star Edward "Whitey" Ford was on the mound. When asked before the game which Pirates batters might give him the most trouble, Whitey Ford had answered, "Groat and Clemente."[5]

Ford gave up only four hits, one of them a single by Clemente. Unable to score any runs, the Pirates gave the New York pitcher a four-hit shutout. The Yankees scored six runs in the bottom of the first, and Bobby Richardson hit a grand slam in the fourth inning to chalk up a 10–0 victory.

Pittsburgh hoped to even the series the following day. The Pirates took a 3–1 lead in the fifth inning. Although Clemente struck out in his first two trips to the plate, he then hit a single to right field in the sixth inning. That was his fifth hit in four games. He had also made eight plays in the field so far without committing an error. Pittsburgh held on for a 3–2 victory.

In game five, the New York crowd watched the Pirates beat the Yankees 5–2. Pittsburgh's victory was helped by Clemente's grounder to the infield in the third inning, which scored Dick Groat. Harvey Haddix was the starting pitcher for Pittsburgh, giving up only five hits, before Roy Face came on in the seventh inning to hold on to the lead.

Pittsburgh needed only one more win to become the World Series champions. Yet back at Forbes Field for game six, they took another beating. Whitey Ford kept Pittsburgh scoreless, holding them to only seven hits—two of which were Clemente's. He hit a single to right field in the first inning and another to center field in the sixth. Arthur Daley of *The New York Times* wrote that in the outfield, Clemente "seemed to do more throwing than any other Pirate. . . . So many hits whistled into his territory that he was forever firing the ball back into the infield."[6] In spite of Clemente's efforts, the Yankees racked up seventeen hits and twelve runs that day, while the Pirates remained scoreless.

With the series tied at three games apiece, the stage was set for what some consider the most exciting game seven ever played. The statistics favored the Yankees, who had so far outscored the Pirates 46–17 and gotten 78 hits to Pittsburgh's 52.

"I really, sincerely believe the Yankees had a better club than we did, overall talent," said Mazeroski, who

Clemente had a hit in every game of the two World Series in which he played.

would hit .320 for the Pirates during the series. "But I didn't consider they were more capable of winning just because of the nature of our club. The club never gave up, and everybody was very capable of doing the job they had to do. And it just seems like things happened."[7]

The Pirates took an early 4–0 lead, holding the Yankees to only one hit in the first four innings. Home runs by Bill Skowron and Yogi Berra helped put New York ahead 7–4 in the top of the eighth inning. When the Pirates came up in the bottom of the eighth inning, Bill Virdon hit a sharp ground ball toward the shortstop. The ball took a bad hop and struck Yankee infielder Tony Kubek in the throat, knocking him down. Kubek, who was sent to the hospital with a bruised larynx, later said, "It happened so quickly that I couldn't even raise my glove in self-defense."[8]

The Pirates now had runners on first and second. Dick Groat hit a single that allowed Gino Cimoli to score from second. With one out to go in the inning, Clemente hit a feeble ground ball between the pitcher's mound and first base. Angry, Clemente ran as hard as he could—even though the chance of safely reaching first base seemed remote. The first baseman ran over to grab it, then waited for the pitcher, Jim Coates, to cover the base and receive the catch. But Clemente beat Coates to first base and was safe. Virdon scored on Clemente's single, bringing the score to 7–6 with the Pirates down by a run.

When catcher Hal Smith came up to the plate, he belted a home run. The Pirates now led the Yankees 9–7. New York came back in the ninth inning to tie the game. When the Pirates came to bat in the bottom of the inning, Bill Mazeroski stepped up to the plate. Facing Yankee pitcher Ralph Terry, Mazeroski slammed the second pitch over the left field wall, giving the Pirates the win. "I didn't think it was going to clear the fence," Terry said. ". . . It was one of the most dramatic home runs in the history of the game."[9]

As Mazeroski scored the winning run in the 1960 World Series, fans rushed onto the field.

When the game ended, the Pirates and thousands of fans ran onto the field.

"Half of Forbes Field was waiting for me," said Mazeroski.[10] It seemed as if the entire city of Pittsburgh was celebrating. Bridges and tunnels had to be closed to incoming traffic because of the masses of people flooding the streets. Hotels would not allow anyone in their lobbies without room keys. By morning, there would be $50,000 worth of destruction to the city from all the partying.

That same year, Dick Groat was voted the National League's Most Valuable Player (MVP) by baseball journalists. The award is usually given to the player who has the most outstanding individual season, or to the player who helps lead his team to a championship. Although Groat's .325 average was better than Clemente's .314, Clemente had batted in ninety-four runs to Groat's fifty. Clemente came in eighth in the ranking and was very bitter about it.[12] Furious that he had finished so low in the voting, Clemente never wore his World Series ring.

> *Clemente was the favorite of many Pirates' fans, but in game seven of the 1960 World Series, it was Mazeroski's turn to revel in the spotlight.*

Clemente was not feeling like a winner.

All-Star

Clemente had helped the Pirates win the World Series, but he did not feel like a winner. The fact that he had not been seriously considered for the 1960 National League Most Valuable Player award upset him. When the 1961 season opened, Clemente was determined to prove that he was worthy of the title.

One of the first changes Clemente made was switching to a heavier bat. He hoped the additional weight would allow him to hit more powerfully to right field and also help control his swing. Clemente continued to work with batting coach George Sisler, and the efforts paid off. By the end of April, he was hitting .323. When the All-Star votes were announced two

> **"I feel I should get the credit I deserve."**[1]
> —Clemente

months later, Clemente was the top choice for the National League right fielder.

Clemente's average had climbed to .357 by the time of the All-Star Game in July. At that time, two All-Star Games were held each year. One took place in San Francisco's Candlestick Park and the other in Boston's Fenway Park. The first All-Star Game of 1961 saw the National League out-hitting the American League 11–4. Yet the game was tied at 3–3 after nine innings. The American League scored a run in the top of the tenth on a throwing error by Ken Boyer. In the bottom of the inning, Hank Aaron of the Milwaukee Braves singled, and San Francisco Giant Willie Mays doubled.

Then Clemente stepped up to the plate. He smacked a single into right field that scored both Aaron and Mays and won the game for the National League. Even though Clemente spurned his 1960 World Series ring, he wore his 1961 All-Star ring with pride. Danny Murtaugh, who was the National League All-Star manager, had kept Clemente in the entire game.

In the locker room afterward, Clemente saw that all the sports writers

Increasing Diversity

By the 1961 All-Star Game, seven of the American League's ten top hitters were African American, along with the four top home-run hitters. In the National League, 17 percent of the players were African American. The All-Star team was composed of 36 percent black players.

had gathered around Willie Mays. He heard Mays telling the reporters to talk to Clemente—after all, it was his hit that won the game. Yet for the most part, Clemente was ignored.

Clemente played exceptionally throughout the 1961 season, although the Pirates would wind up finishing in sixth place. With some of his teammates good-naturedly nicknaming him "No Votes" because of the MVP voting the previous year, Clemente hit .351 for the season. He had 201 hits, 30 doubles, and 23 home runs. His numbers earned him the 1961 National League batting championship. Clemente was the first native Puerto Rican ever to win that major league title.

The batting title meant a lot to Clemente. Not only had he set out to be the best ballplayer in the league in 1961, but he also felt pride in his accomplishments as a Puerto Rican. His fellow countrymen were equally proud. Like many Puerto Ricans, Clemente had loved baseball from the time he was young. Back then, Babe Ruth was considered the best player of all.

"But Babe Ruth was an American player," said Clemente. "What we needed was a Puerto Rican player they could say that about, someone to look up to and try to equal."[2] Clemente was giving the Puerto Rican baseball fans someone to look up to—and they adored him.

Another Puerto Rican ballplayer, Orlando Cepeda, hit 46 home runs for the Giants and captured the National League home run crown that year, as well as the RBI championship with 142. Together, the two

Extra batting practice paid off for Clemente, who became the first Puerto Rican–born player to earn the National League batting championship.

Puerto Rican athletes had won the National League's Triple Crown.

In 1961 Clemente finished fourth in the MVP voting and was honored by some local organizations in Pittsburgh, such as the charitable sports group the Dapper Dan Club. Yet he felt his greatest honor was the reception waiting for him when he flew home in the off-season. Stepping off the plane at the airport in San Juan, Clemente and Cepeda were greeted by eighteen thousand fans. The two ballplayers then traveled to Sixto Escobar Stadium, where five thousand more fans welcomed them. The response of his countrymen made Clemente feel proud and joyful.

The 1962 season did not start off as brightly for Clemente. Ten pounds lighter when he showed up at spring training, he was having stomach troubles and looked tired. Clemente maintained that he was usually dealing with several injuries or physical problems every time he stepped onto the field.

Former Pirates pitcher Nelson Briles said, "Roberto used to say, 'People pay to see me perform. If I go out there 75 percent, I'm not giving them the performance they paid to see.' What Roberto didn't understand was that his 75 percent was better than other guys' 100 percent."[3]

Clemente began the season hitting .256. Yet in spite of not feeling his best, he went on to hit .312 that year, with twenty-eight doubles, nine triples, and ten home runs. The Pirates took fourth place in the league. After the regular season, Clemente returned to Puerto Rico to play winter league ball. His ties to his native land were as strong as ever. He had adopted the children of both a sister and brother who had died, which gave him an added financial responsibility. He invested some of his money in four small homes in Puerto Rico, which he rented out for $90 a month.

Clemente also began studying chiropractics, a type of therapy that involves manually adjusting the spine. He wanted to open a clinic in Puerto Rico to treat patients who suffered from back problems.

Before the start of the 1963 season, the Pirates' general manager Joe Brown traded infielders Dick Groat and Don Hoak for Juan "Pancho" Herrera, Julio Gotay, Ted Savage, and Don Cardwell. The Pirates also acquired Manny Mota from the San Francisco Giants and Jim Pagliaroni, a catcher, from the Boston Red Sox.

The season was disastrous for the Pirates, with the team finishing in eighth place. Clemente hit .320 for the year. His health was holding steady, but his temper was not. He had numerous arguments with the team's manager, Danny Murtaugh. Once, during a road trip to the West Coast, Clemente became sick after a meal of shrimp and steak. He had to have his stomach pumped. The next day he told Murtaugh he was too weak to play, but Murtaugh kept his name in the lineup. After Clemente repeated that he was not feeling well, he was benched for three straight games. At other times, Murtaugh fined Clemente up to $650 for his behavior.

Clemente became angry when he believed he was not treated fairly. One day in May, he was called out on a play at first base. The next day he saw a newspaper photograph proving that he had been safe by more than three feet.[4] He was furious. A couple of weeks later, Clemente was again called out as he headed for first. He argued the call and then bumped—or hit—the umpire twice. Clemente was thrown out of the game. He was further punished by the National League with a $250 fine and a five-day suspension.

Clemente said his run-in with the umpire was an accident, that he hit the man with an open palm, not his fist. He stated that he was only trying to get away from first base coach Ron Northey, who had come between them. National League

> **"I'm a very quiet, shy person, though you writers might not believe it because I shout sometimes."[5]**
>
> **—Clemente**

president Warren Giles, however, called the incident "the most serious reported to our office in several years."[6]

Still, Clemente won his third straight Gold Glove that year. Gold Gloves are awarded to the best fielders at each position. His .320 batting average placed him second in the National League.

When Clemente returned to Puerto Rico that winter, he met the woman who would become his wife. Like

Clemente, Vera Christina Zabala came from Carolina. She had attended the University of Puerto Rico for three years and then taken a job as secretary at a bank. Clemente was out shopping when he noticed her. Later that day, he told his mother that he had seen the woman he was going to marry.

Soon after Clemente found out Vera's name, he called her at work to invite her out to lunch. Traditions in Puerto Rico were more conservative than those in the United States. At that time, if a Puerto Rican man wanted to date a woman, he could not approach her directly. Clemente had been so interested in meeting Vera Zabala that he had forgotten this custom. Zabala, who came from an old-fashioned family, did not accept his invitation to lunch.

Vera Zabala
Vera did not know much about baseball when she started dating Clemente, so she asked her friends to teach her everything they knew. When Vera went to the San Juan ball field for the first time to see Clemente, she had hoped to see him make dazzling plays in the field. However, it rained and the game was postponed.

Clemente did not give up. When he learned that Zabala was going to a party one night, he made sure to stop by. In that way, he could approach her in a crowd of people and talk to her. They went on their first date to a baseball stadium in San Juan. Zabala did not know that Clemente was a famous ball player. She found out soon after, when he visited her at the bank and crowds of people swarmed around him.

As the 1964 season got off the ground, Clemente was hitting .398. He seemed to be feeling well and sleeping better. As he approached the age of thirty, he was taking a leadership role in the Pirates' clubhouse. By the time the year was over, he had achieved career highs in hits (211), doubles (40), and walks (51). Although the Pirates finished in a tie for sixth place, Clemente won the National League batting title. He thought he would be among the top candidates for the MVP award. However, the honors went to St. Louis Cardinal Ken Boyer. Clemente came in ninth in the voting.

On top of this disappointment, Clemente was not selected for the 1964 All-Star team. The outfielders chosen by United Press International journalists were Willie Mays, Mickey Mantle, and Billy Williams of the Cubs. Clemente was considered the top defensive right fielder in the game, and his batting average for 1964 had been .339. But unlike the other three players, he was not a top home run hitter.

Roberto Clemente and Vera Zabala were married on November 14, 1964, and made their home in a wealthy section of Rio Piedras. Over the years, they would go on to have three boys—Roberto Jr., Luis, and Enrique.

During the off-season in 1964, Clemente began some baseball clinics for underprivileged children in Puerto Rico. He worked personally with the youngsters, encouraging them to try their hardest and learn the

Newlyweds Roberto and Vera Clemente pose for a photo on their wedding day.

basics. Clemente did not start these clinics to make money, and he received no pay for his efforts. His goal was to help Puerto Rican youth, and he would continue the clinics in future years. He was beginning to think ahead to his retirement, when he hoped to start a sports city for the young people of Puerto Rico.

Clemente also agreed to manage his winter league team, the San Juan Senators, for a short time during the off-season of 1964. Although he hoped his role as manager would last only a few games, he took over the job for the entire winter league season. The team finished fourth in the league.

Most Valuable Player

While Clemente was cutting his grass in Puerto Rico, he was seriously injured when his lawnmower propelled a rock into his leg. In the hospital, doctors removed a blood clot from his right thigh. The surgeons also found a tear in the thigh muscle. Clemente remained in the hospital for a week and was ordered to spend the rest of the 1964 off-season recovering. During this time, a case of malaria sent Clemente back to the hospital. He lost twenty pounds and missed the start of the Pirates' 1965 spring training.

Harry Walker had taken over as the Pirates' new manager. Walker, who had played in the National League years earlier, was nicknamed "The Hat" because he had a habit of adjusting his cap after every pitch.

Although Clemente was still weak at the start of the season, he played right field every day. His hitting was below average, so Walker decided to put him on the

Clemente looks ready for a hit in this game against the Chicago Cubs in May 1965.

bench for a while until he regained his strength. Tired as he was, Clemente was upset about not being played. He angrily talked to Walker and by May was taking more trips to the plate.

As the season progressed, Clemente's hitting improved. By the All-Star break, he and Willie Mays had the highest averages in the National League. Still, Clemente came in third among league right fielders when fans voted for the All-Star team. He was picked by National League All-Star manager Gene Mauch as a reserve outfielder, which meant he would not be in the starting lineup. As soon as Clemente heard this, he stated that he would absolutely not play in the game.[1] If the fans did not think enough of him to vote him onto the team, he did not want to play at all. After Walker had a talk with Clemente, the ballplayer wound up playing the game.

Clemente hit well throughout the summer. His batting average reached a high of .345 but eventually settled down to .329 for the season. He also won his third National League batting championship, joining Hall of Fame athletes Rogers Hornsby, Stan Musial, Honus Wagner, and Paul Waner.

When the 1966 season opened, Clemente faced two challenges. The first involved new center fielder Matty Alou, who had come from the San Francisco Giants with a batting average of .231. Alou spoke Spanish and only a little English, so the Pirates manager asked Clemente to help him improve his hitting. Alou seemed to be hitting mainly to right field; Walker wanted him to hit to left.

Clemente began working with Alou during spring training. Standing near third base, Clemente would tell Alou to hit the ball to him. They did this over and over until Alou developed the habit of hitting down the third-base line. His batting average showed a marked improvement, rising 111 points by the end of season.

The other challenge Clemente faced was more personal. Although he was aware that Clemente was an outstanding hitter, Walker wanted to see more power at the plate—more home runs and more RBIs. Clemente had averaged only ten home runs a year in the major league, and that average was largely helped by his twenty-three home runs in 1961 and sixteen in 1960.

Matty Alou

Matty Alou played for the San Francisco Giants from 1960 to 1965. He then played for Pittsburgh from 1966 to 1972 before eventually joining Oakland, New York, and San Diego. He had his best year in 1966 when he led the National League in batting at .342. Three years later, he led the National League in hits and doubles. Alou was known for his excellent bat control: He hit over .300 seven times in his career. Alou's two brothers—Felipe and Jesus—were also major league ball players. Matty was faster and a better hitter than either of his brothers, with a lifetime career average of .307.

Walker was asking for 115 RBIs each season, while Clemente had been averaging only sixty-five RBIs. Clemente sought the help of some of Pirates' coaches and pushed himself to become a more powerful hitter.

Still, the 1966 season began slowly for Clemente. By the end of June, he had hit only three home runs and batted in just seventeen runs. Then things began to pick up. Clemente was selected for the National League's All-Star outfield. His two hits—a double and a single—helped his team beat the American League. Throughout the season, Clemente went on hitting streaks that lasted up to seventeen games. Several times he got four hits in a game. On September 2 at Forbes Field, Clemente reached the two-thousand-hit mark against the Chicago Cubs.

Clemente believed that one reason for the improvement in his batting was that the sand in the batter's box at Forbes Field had been replaced with clay. Clemente had been asking for clay for years, convinced that it would give him a firmer footing at the plate. Now he was finally able to dig his feet in.

Although the Pirates finished third in the league in 1966, Clemente had a remarkable year. Walker had asked him to hit 25 home runs and 115 RBIs. Clemente had delivered twenty home runs and 119 RBIs. His average was .317, which placed him fourth in the National League. While Clemente did not win another batting championship that year, he won the award that meant the most to him: Most Valuable Player for the

National League. Members of the Baseball Writers Association had ranked Clemente slightly higher than Dodgers pitcher Sandy Koufax. "It's the highest honor a player can hope for, but I was expecting it," said Clemente. ". . . I had the best season of my career and I was confident that the sports writers would vote for me. I am thankful they did."[2]

Pirates' manager Harry Walker said, "He won the MVP because he did so many little things. He did the things so many stars don't: hustling on routine ground balls, breaking up double plays, taking the extra base."[3]

Clemente keeps his eye on the ball of his 2,000th career hit, September 2, 1966. After what he called "the best season of my career," Clemente was voted Most Valuable Player for the National League.

On top of that honor, Clemente was also voted National League Player of the Year by *The Sporting News*. The ballplayers had been polled, and they had chosen Clemente.

Clemente signed a new contract during the off-season for $100,000. Not only was he the first Pirate in history to earn that amount, but he joined only five other ballplayers who had salaries that large: Willie Mays, Hank Aaron, Mickey Mantle, and Frank Robinson.

Anthony Bartirome, a trainer, told a story about Clemente and money: One day in Pittsburgh, Clemente—who was often late—hurried onto the field. He quickly handed Bartirome an envelope. It contained a check, and he wanted Bartirome to hold on to it. Bartirome stuffed the envelope into his pocket alongside the bandages and gauze pads he kept there. Then both men forgot all about it. A week later, Clemente asked for the envelope. After digging around in his pocket, Bartirome found it. When Clemente looked inside, Bartirome could see a $25,000 check. He had no idea he had been carrying such a huge sum in his pocket.[4]

That winter in Puerto Rico was not an easy one for Clemente. His brother Osvaldo died after a long illness. Only weeks later, his brother Vicente died, followed by Clemente's aunt. "Osvaldo was the head of the family, and I sort of had to take over for him," said Clemente. "We are a close family, and it was sad for all of us."[5]

Clemente passed his time working on a farm he owned just outside San Juan. He also opened a restaurant called El Carrertero, which means "The man who leads the ox-drawn cart."[6] The business did well for a few years, but then it began to fail. Clemente finally had to close El Carrertero, losing thousands of dollars.

When the 1967 baseball season opened, there were

many positive changes for Clemente. First baseman Donn Clendenon said Clemente appeared to be a new man. He seemed to have lost a lot of the anger he had carried around in the early years of his career. Now Clemente worked on keeping peace among the players, the manager, and the Pirates administration. A loner when he first arrived in Pittsburgh, Clemente now went out with the other players and seemed more comfortable with himself and his team. Clemente was recognized as a superstar, and he felt appreciated.

In July the Pirates traveled to New York City. The visit occurred at the same time as a film crew's trip to Shea Stadium, home of the Mets. The film crew was working on a baseball scene for the movie *The Odd Couple*. Producers asked players from both the Pirates and the Mets to appear in the movie.

Clemente was offered $100 a day to take part in the film. However, he misunderstood what kind of movie it was. Clemente thought the crew was shooting a documentary for children. In fact the movie was a comedy, and the script called for Clemente to hit into a triple play—three outs would be made after he hit the ball.

That evening, when Clemente told Matty Alou about his role in the movie, Alou laughed. He suggested that Clemente should be paid at least $1,000. The more Clemente thought about it, the angrier he became. Throughout his career, he had felt that he was not being taken seriously—and here was more proof that he was right. He was being underpaid as well as being asked to play the part of a ballplayer whose hit leads to three outs for his team.

By the next day, Clemente was sure he was being cheated and his baseball abilities insulted. He informed the film crew that he would not appear in the movie. Clemente then walked over to the batting cage and took a few swings. One ball sailed 440 feet over the fence in left center field. Clemente shouted to a cameraman, "Hey, take a picture of that home run and put it in your stinkin' picture. You can have it for nothin'."[7]

The Pirates 1967 season was a disappointing one, with the team finishing in sixth place. But statistically, 1967 was another strong year for thirty-three-year-old Clemente. He hit 23 home runs and batted in 110 runs. His batting reached a career high of .357 and won Clemente his fourth batting title. At that point in history, only five other players had won more titles: Ty Cobb, Honus Wagner, Rogers Hornsby, Stan Musial, and Ted Williams. Clemente and Harry Heilman were tied at four.

> **"I try to catch everything in the ballpark."[8]**
>
> **—Clemente**

Clemente's 209 base hits were also the best in the league. During one particular game, on May 15, Clemente seemed to be a one-man show against the Cincinnati Reds. Although the Pirates lost 8–7 in ten innings, Clemente hit three home runs and a double. He had been responsible for all of the Pirates' runs.

Hall of Famer Harold "Pie" Traynor declared Clemente to be the top right fielder in National League history. Hank Aaron, speaking of his admiration for Clemente, called him "great."[9]

When Harry Walker was quoted that season in *Time* magazine, he called Clemente "Just the best player in baseball, that's all."[10]

That opinion also seemed to be the consensus of the other major league general managers. In March 1968, *Sport* magazine asked them to name the greatest player in baseball. The majority voted for Clemente.

Before the regular 1968 season began, Clemente was once again at his home in Puerto Rico—and once again had to deal with a serious injury. Just before spring training one day, Clemente was lifting himself up a wall by climbing up an iron railing at the back of his house. The rail he was holding on to broke, and Clemente fell down a hill and rolled about one hundred feet. He was fortunate that the four-foot-long bar did not fall on his chest and crush him. He landed on the back of his neck, and his right shoulder was hurt in the fall. It was an injury that would bother him all season.

> **"I'm lucky to be alive."[11]**
>
> **—Clemente**

The painful tear in Clemente's shoulder was inconsequential in light of major news that stunned the nation at the start of the season: On April 4, 1968, civil rights leader Martin Luther King, Jr., was assassinated.

Clemente had met Dr. King a few years earlier in Puerto Rico. He believed the Pirates should acknowledge the loss of this great man. The Pirates had more African-American players at that time than any other team in baseball. Led by Clemente, the Pirates decided they did not want to play their final exhibition game on Sunday, nor would they play their regular season games on Monday and Tuesday against the Houston Astros. King was to be buried on Tuesday. There was much debate between the Pirates' and Astros' organizations, but finally it was agreed—the Pirates first game would be on a Wednesday.

By this time, Clemente had become a leader among the players. He frequently called meetings and, using much humor, urged his teammates to try harder and give it their all. Sometimes Clemente even put on a wig and pretended to be a judge. Standing on a bucket, he would call players up to his "bench," tell them what they had done wrong, and make them pay a fine.[12]

The team finished in sixth place that year, and Clemente's numbers took a huge dive. He was not invited to the All-Star Game, and only through a huge effort late in the season was he able to pull up his average to .291. The shoulder injury hurt him every day, and Clemente declared that he would stop playing baseball the following year if he could not find a way to get rid of the pain.

All winter at his home in Puerto Rico, Clemente toyed with the idea of retiring, but his love for the game brought him back for another season. Meanwhile, the Pirates had gone through some managerial changes. Danny Murtaugh had returned mid-season during 1967 and replaced Walker. In 1968, Larry Shepard came in, and Alex Grammas served as manager in 1969.

Clemente had become a leader among the players on his team.

The Pirates had also moved their Florida spring training location from Fort Myers to Bradenton. Although Clemente felt well at the start of spring training, he smashed into a fence in right field in mid-March while running down a fly ball. This time he hurt his left shoulder. Another injury came at the start of the season when he pulled a thigh muscle after chasing a foul ball and crashing into a wall.

On top of these injuries, Clemente had an unusual experience while he was in San Diego, California, on a road trip. He walked to a restaurant one day and ordered a box of fried chicken. As he headed back to his hotel, a car with four men pulled up next to him. A man holding a gun ordered Clemente to get in.

After driving about fifteen minutes, the car stopped in an abandoned mountainous area. The men ordered Clemente to take off his clothes, down to his underwear. They forced him to hand over his wallet, which held $250, and his All-Star Game ring. Clemente was sure the men were going to shoot him and toss his body in the woods.

Hoping the men were baseball fans, Clemente told them he was a ballplayer. After he showed them his membership card in the Baseball Players' Association, the men returned Clemente's wallet, ring, and clothes. Then they dropped him off three blocks away from his hotel. As Clemente started to walk to the hotel, he heard the car coming his way. Had the thieves changed their minds and decided to kill him after all? The car pulled up next to Clemente—and the men held out the box of chicken. They were returning that, too.

Although some players and fans did not believe Clemente's story, the records of the San Diego police department have the details on file just as Clemente reported them that day.[13]

Clemente's hitting picked up as the season progressed. Many people wondered if he would reach the milestone of three thousand hits. He had already hit more than 2,400. Clemente did not think it was possible. He was thirty-four years old and did not expect to be playing long enough to get another six hundred hits.

Clemente finished the 1969 season with a .345 average. There was a rumor near the end of the season that he might be traded for a younger player. This did not happen. He stayed with the Pirates and would once again help the team make history.

"I want to be remembered as a ballplayer who gave all he had to give," said Clemente.

9

World Champions
. . . Again

As the 1970 season began, Clemente was wondering out loud whether he might be able to collect three thousand hits before his career ended. He had now been playing in the major leagues for fifteen years. His wife, Vera, and their three children would watch from their box seat at the stadium. As for the Pittsburgh fans, they loved him more than ever.

Clemente's personality had been something of a mystery through the years. His temper and his arguments with managers and sportswriters were well known. Yet for every person who claimed he was hotheaded and arrogant, there were even more who vouched for his kindness and generosity.

Many people who met Clemente had their own story to tell. After a game in Houston one day, Clemente was signing autographs. He began talking to a woman named Loretta Miller, her two sons, and two of her friends.

Clemente needed a ride to the Marriott Hotel, where he was staying. Miller offered to drive him. At the hotel, Miller's sons rushed into the lobby to ask other Pirates players for their autographs. Clemente followed the boys to make sure they were all right. "He is really one of the nicest men I've ever met," Miller said later.[1]

New York Post columnist Milton Gross once had a misunderstanding with Clemente over a newspaper story. Clemente wrote an angry letter to Gross, claiming that his column had not been accurate. When Gross confronted Clemente and asked him to point out the problem, Clemente admitted that he had not actually read the column. A friend had told him about it. Gross suggested that Clemente read the story himself and then see if he felt differently. Clemente did . . . and he apologized to Gross.

> **Every year, the fans loved Clemente even more.**

Clemente had always had a special interest in helping young people. He was asked if he would take part in a television film aimed at warning young people about the danger of taking drugs. Clemente agreed, but he was not happy that the film would be made in English, and not in Spanish as well. The film producers explained that they could not make a Spanish version because they did not have anyone who could translate the script. Clemente volunteered and spent his own time working on translating the English into Spanish.

Meanwhile, the Pirates started out the 1970 season slowly but soon got back on track. By mid-season, they were in first place in the National League East.

On July 16 the Pirates took the field of their new home, Three Rivers Stadium, located where the Allegheny and Monongahela Rivers join to form the Ohio River. The artificial-turf stadium could seat 48,044. A ceremony was held at the new ballpark on July 24. But it was not to honor the stadium—it was to honor Clemente. On Roberto Clemente Night, the athlete walked onto the field before the game and received a standing ovation. His family and many friends from Puerto Rico had come for the occasion.

Juan Esteban Jiménez, a young Puerto Rican businessman, decided to do something special for the celebration. He began a project, which he called *Puerto Rico Felicita a Clemente*, which translates as Puerto Rico Congratulates Clemente. Jiménez wanted to get the entire island of Puerto Rico involved in the event, and so he made an enormous scroll for thousands of Puerto Ricans to sign. Jimenez arranged for a group of people to help him collect the signatures and when they were finished, three hundred thousand people had signed the scroll.

Jiménez also wanted to present Clemente with a gift. After thinking it over, he decided the best gift would be to send underprivileged children to the event in Pittsburgh. Then they could see for themselves how much a person could achieve through hard work.

Jiménez accompanied the children on the flight to Pittsburgh.

Clemente was touched by the evening's festivities. "There are things in life that mean the most to me, my family—and the fans in Pittsburgh and Puerto Rico," he tearfully told the crowd.[2] Clemente was given numerous trophies along with such gifts as a television set and a new car. Silver mugs, autographed by all the players, coaches, and manager, were presented on a silver tray. A trust fund was set up to provide for the college education of his three sons. Also, a check for more than $5,000 was made out to the Children's Hospital in Pittsburgh. Clemente liked to visit the youngsters in the hospital when he had free time, and he had asked fans to donate money to the hospital in his name. "He was always thinking of other people," said his friend Phil Dorsey.[4]

> *"There are things in life that mean the most to me, my family—and the fans in Pittsburgh and Puerto Rico."[3]*
>
> *—Clemente*

That night Clemente made two hits and a walk. The hits brought his batting average up to .356.

Several injuries that season often took Clemente out of the lineup. He tried some unusual cures to get himself back on his feet—such as having the trainer rub him down with goat's milk when his back was bothering

A family portrait: Clemente posed with his parents, wife, and sons when he was honored at the opening of Three Rivers Stadium.

him. Even though he played in only 108 games that season, Clemente wound up with a .352 average, the second best of his career.

The Pirates found themselves in first place in September. The team would be facing the Cincinnati Reds in their bid for the National League championship. There were concerns about Clemente's health. There were also concerns about who would umpire the game. The six major league umpires wanted an increase in their play-off salaries from $2,500 to $5,000 and a jump from $6,500 to $10,000 for the World Series. They went on strike, but the owners refused to give them the pay hike. Instead, minor league umpires were hired.

The first game of the league championship went ten innings, with the Reds claiming a 3–0 victory. Clemente struck out in three of his five times at bat.

> ## "He was always thinking of other people."[5]
>
> —Phil Dorsey

The umpires and owners reached an agreement before the start of game two. This did not seem to affect the Pirates, who could manage only five hits in the 3–1 loss to the Reds. Clemente had one of those hits, allowing Dave Cash to score the only Pittsburgh run of the game.

The third game took place at Riverfront Stadium in Cincinnati. The Pirates battled but were losing 3–2 after eight innings. Cincinnati pitcher Wayne Granger got the first two Pittsburgh batters out easily in the top of the ninth. When Clemente came up, he singled. Willie Stargell came up next and also singled. With men on first and third, Al Oliver stepped to the plate and hit an easy ground ball to the second baseman for the third out. The Pirates had lost their bid for the pennant.

That winter in Puerto Rico, Clemente again took on the job of manager for the San Juan Senators. His team finished second in their league with a 37–30 record. Clemente played on the team as well as managing it, and his pinch-hit single in the ninth inning of a play-off game brought in two runs. He also speculated that he might like to try managing the Pirates sometime in the future.

Clemente was thirty-six years old in 1971. Danny Murtaugh, who had come back in 1970 as manager of the Pirates, wanted to keep Clemente healthy through-out the season. He gave Clemente rest whenever possible and did not put him in the lineup every day. Clemente started out slowly, batting only .260 in May. By mid-June, he was hitting well over .300.

Clemente's fielding remained exceptional. "When Clemente was out in the field," Pirate pitcher Steve Blass said years later, "it was like having four outfield-ers."[6] The finest play of Clemente's career may have come during a June 15 game against the Houston Astros at the Astrodome. The Pirates were ahead by one run, and there were two outs in the bottom of the eighth inning. The Astros had a man on first when Bob Watson came up and hit a hard shot down the right-field line. According to spectators at the game, it looked like a sure home run.

Clemente ran toward the wall and leaped into the air, his body extended and his back to home plate. He had to catch the ball before it hit above the yellow line painted on the wall, or it would be ruled a home run. He backhanded the ball and smashed facefirst into the concrete, then fell to the ground. His left ankle, knee, and elbow were hurt when he crashed into the wall. Yet

Clemente held on to the ball. All the fans at the Astrodome stood up to give him a standing ovation. After that, the Pirates hung on to their lead and won the game 3–0.

The 1971 season was a good one for the Pirates and for Clemente personally. He was enjoying spending time with his teammates—both on the field and off. There was one story that Clemente found so funny, he asked to hear it over and over. Anthony Bartirome and some friends had played a practical joke on the team doctor. A life-sized wax statue of Clemente had been created for an event at Three Rivers Stadium. It was fully dressed in a uniform and a baseball cap. When the statue was ready to be stored, Bartirome suggested putting it in the backroom of the clubhouse. The statue was placed on a table and covered with a blanket, leaving only an arm and the face exposed.

> *"When Clemente was out in the field, it was like having four outfielders."* [7]
>
> —Pitcher Steve Blass

Bartirome then called in the team doctor. Clemente had been sick with a virus for several weeks and was still not feeling well. Bartirome asked the doctor to examine Clemente. The backroom was very dark, and the wax statue under the blanket appeared to be the ballplayer.

The doctor asked Clemente how he was feeling.

When he received no answer, the doctor reached over and grabbed Clemente's wrist to take his pulse. The wrist felt cold and waxy. There was no pulse. Thinking Clemente had died, he yelled out, "Oh . . . my God!"[8] Bartirome and his friends enjoyed a hearty laugh.

The Pirates took first place that season in the eastern division of the National League. On September 1, Clemente was part of a historical lineup. Murtaugh called up the following players: Rennie Stennett, second base; Gene Clines, center field; Roberto Clemente, right field; Willie Stargell, left field; Manny Sanguillen,

Clemente's family was proud to see him celebrated in September 1971 at Shea Stadium in New York City.

catcher; Dave Cash, third base; Al Oliver, first base; Jackie Hernandez, shortstop; Dock Ellis, pitcher. For the first time in major league baseball, the lineup was made up entirely of people of color.

In late September, Puerto Ricans from New York and San Juan gathered at Shea Stadium to honor Roberto Clemente. More than forty-four thousand people turned out for the event. Carlos Diaz, owner of a bar in the Bronx, helped organize the event. He had grown up with Clemente, and they used to play softball together. He appreciated Clemente's generosity as well as his athletic skill. Diaz was also chairman of the Hispanic Association Development of Youth organization. At one point, he asked Clemente for a donation of baseball gloves for the children. "Although I had only asked for one dozen gloves, he sent four dozen," said Diaz later. "He never forgot his people."[9]

The Pirates faced the San Francisco Giants at Candlestick Park for the first game of the league championship. Steve Blass of Pittsburgh was pitted against San Francisco pitcher Gaylord Perry. The Pirates were down by three runs in the top of the seventh inning. Al Oliver singled, bringing in two more runs and cutting the Giants' lead to one run. But no more runs would be scored in the game. The Giants won, 5–4.

In game two, the Pirates found themselves holding a 4–2 lead going into the sixth inning. With two outs and the bases loaded, Willie Mays came to the plate. Mays batted a line drive into right-center field. Clemente raced for the ball and caught it, largely because he had instinctively decided to move five steps to his right only seconds earlier. Murtaugh later said that Clemente could never have made the play if he had not changed his position. The Pirates went on to win game two and then traveled across the country to Three Rivers Stadium for the rest of the series.

The Pirates fought hard to secure a 2–1 victory in game three. Now they needed only one more win to gain a spot in the World Series. Game four seesawed back and forth between the

> *"He never forgot his people."*[10]
>
> —*Carlos Diaz*

two teams. The Giants grabbed an early 5–2 lead, but then the Pirates came back to tie it at 5–5. Clemente got his third RBI of the game in the bottom of the sixth inning and a home run later that inning, putting the Pirates ahead 9–5. They held on to the lead by the end of the game and celebrated their first World Series appearance since 1960.

Clemente had done well in the playoffs with his outstanding fielding, four RBIs, and .333 average at the plate. Although the Pirates had won the National League East division by seven games and defeated the Giants 3–1 for the pennant, the Baltimore Orioles had just swept the American League for the third time in a row. They were the first team—other than the Yankees— to win three straight American League titles in forty years. Besides completing their third one-hundred-win season, the Orioles were only the second team in major league baseball to have four pitchers in their rotation who each had won twenty games—Dave McNally, Jim Palmer, Mike Cuellar, and Pat Dobson.

The 1971 World Series opened on Saturday, October 9, at Memorial Stadium in Baltimore, Maryland. The Pirates jumped out to an early lead by getting three runs off McNally in the second inning. McNally did not allow any more hits after that. The Pirates had been able to get only three hits in their 5–3 loss—and two of those hits had come off Clemente's bat.

> **"I gave everything I had to the game."**[11]
>
> **—Clemente**

The Orioles easily defeated the Pirates 11–3 in the second game. The series then moved to Pittsburgh. Steve Blass, on the mound for the Pirates in game three, allowed only three hits. Clemente batted in a run in the first inning with a grounder to the infield. A three-run home run by Bob Robertson in the seventh inning gave the Pirates a 5–1 victory.

Game four, on October 13, was the first World Series game ever played at night. Baltimore scored early, with three runs in the first inning. The Pirates came back to tie it at 3–3 and finally went ahead by a run to even the series at two games apiece.

The young Pittsburgh pitcher Nelson Briles came up with an unexpected two-hitter that gave the Pirates a

4–0 win in the fifth game. The Pirates were now one game away from winning the World Series.

In game six, played in Baltimore, Clemente came up in the second inning with a home run, but the game was tied 2–2 by the end of nine innings. In the tenth inning, the Orioles scored to win it 3–2.

Game seven would be the deciding game. Steve Blass faced Mike Cuellar. Both teams were scoreless until the fourth inning, when Clemente hit a two-out solo home run to left center. This put the Pirates ahead 1–0. José Pagan doubled in the eighth, scoring Willie

As Clemente rounds third on his way home, he is congratulated by third-base coach Frank Oceak. This was the winning game of the 1971 World Series.

Stargell. The Pirates needed only six outs to win the title. The Orioles scored in the eighth, but it was not enough. Helped by Clemente's amazing hitting, fielding, running, and powerful throwing, the Pirates held on to win 2–1. They had won the World Series!

Clemente, having racked up twelve hits in twenty-nine trips to the plate, ended the series with a .414 average and the honor of being the World Series Most Valuable Player. He had commented earlier in the series, "Nobody does anything better than me in baseball."[12] Finally, everyone else seemed to agree with him. Don Buford of the Orioles said, "When a guy gets older, you see him slow up a bit, but not Clemente. His reflexes are still great."[13]

> *"This World Series is the greatest thing that ever happened to me in baseball."*[14]
>
> —*Clemente*

Clemente stood on the podium along with Steve Blass, Danny Murtaugh, and broadcaster Bob Prince. Baseball Commissioner Bowie Kuhn presented them with the World Series Championship trophy. Prince congratulated Clemente, and the ballplayer gave a short speech in Spanish as he looked at the television cameras. Directing his words to his mother and father, Clemente said, "In this, the proudest moment of my life, I ask for your blessing."[15]

Clemente sat happily in the locker room as everyone celebrated. He took special joy in seeing Jackie Hernández and Willie Stargell—a black Latino and a black American—enter the clubhouse with their arms around each other. Clemente felt he had helped bring players of different backgrounds together.[16]

Clemente had hit safely in all seven games, with two home runs and four RBIs, and he was in the national spotlight. Local newspapers and television stations focused their coverage on hometown baseball games, so people throughout the country had little opportunity to see Clemente play. Because he was not regarded as a power hitter, he had not garnered the attention given to home run hitters such as Willie Mays and Hank Aaron. For Clemente, the 1971 World Series changed everything. Now, in honor of Clemente's outstanding play, the organist at Three Rivers Stadium played "Jesus Christ Superstar" whenever Clemente came to bat.

Recapping Clemente's World Series performance, baseball writer Roger Angell said, "Clemente played a kind of baseball that none of us had ever seen before— throwing and running and hitting at something close to the level of absolute perfection."[17]

A Lifetime of Accomplishments

Clemente was greeted as a hero when he flew to Puerto Rico in October 1971. The airport was mobbed with family and friends. "For a month and a half, my wife and I couldn't sleep," said Clemente. "Our house was like a museum—people flocking down the street, ringing our bell day and night, walking through our room."[1]

A few months later, administrators at the Catholic University of Puerto Rico announced they would be awarding Clemente an honorary doctorate in education. According to the university's president, Francisco Carreras, it was the first time the school had honored an athlete in this way.[2]

When spring training began the following year, Clemente was intent on reaching three thousand hits before his retirement. Mets outfielder Tommie Agee was confident that Clemente would succeed. "If Clemente can walk, Clemente can hit," he said.[3]

As interested as he was in continuing to play baseball, Clemente also wanted to pursue his dream of building a sports city in Puerto Rico. He called it "the biggest ambition in my life."[4] The plan called for a place where children of all economic backgrounds could stay for a length of time and learn a variety of sports. Clemente believed that getting children involved in sports might be one way of preventing them from turning to drugs when they got older.

"I get kids together and talk about the importance of sports, the importance of being a good citizen, the importance of respecting their mother and father," he said. "Then we go to the ballfield and I show them some techniques of playing baseball."[5]

Clemente wanted his sports city to have three baseball fields, a swimming pool, basketball and tennis courts, and a lake for other recreational sports. He intended to raise about $2.5 million in federal funds. "I don't want anything for myself," he said, "but through me I can help lots of people."[6]

A baseball players' strike cut out the first seven games of the Pirates' season. Clemente was 118 hits away from his goal. By mid-June, 1972, he had 1,275 RBIs, the most in the history of the Pirates organization. On September 2, Clemente got the 2,971st hit of his career. He had now moved past Honus Wagner as the all-time hit leader on the Pirates. When Clemente reached hit 2,999 against the Phillies in Philadelphia, the Pirates' current manager, Bill Virdon, pulled Clemente from

With 1,275 runs batted in, Clemente was the Pirates' all-time RBI leader in June 1972.

the game. Although the season was nearing an end, Virdon wanted Clemente's three thousandth hit to take place at Three Rivers Stadium in Pittsburgh.

The following night, the Pirates were home against the New York Mets. Tom Seaver was on the mound for New York. Clemente hit a single that bounced off the glove of second baseman Ken Boswell. Instantly, the scoreboard lit up. The fans roared, and the umpire handed the ball to Clemente. Then suddenly the scoreboard lit up again—the play had been ruled an error, not a hit. Clemente believed he had gotten a legitimate hit, but the celebration would have to wait. Officially, he was still at 2,999.

The following day, September 30, Jon Matlack took the mound for the Mets. Clemente came up in the first inning and struck out. He came up for the second time in the bottom of the fourth inning, and Matlack threw the first pitch for a strike. The second pitch was a curve ball, which Clemente hit to the gap in left-center field. He scrambled to second base for a double, and the thirteen thousand fans roared. He had finally done it. Roberto Clemente had become the eleventh major league player to reach three thousand hits. He was also the first Latin American player in history to reach the mark.

As the crowd gave him a standing ovation, Clemente stood on second base and lifted his helmet as a way of saying thank you. Then one of the umpires handed Clemente the ball. When he took the field in the top

When this 1972 swing sent the ball flying, Clemente became the eleventh player in major league history—and the first Latino—to achieve 3,000 hits.

of the fifth inning, the crowd gave him yet another standing ovation. No one had any way of knowing that it would be Clemente's last regular season hit of his career. No one could predict that tragedy awaited Clemente only three months later.

Clemente did not play in the last three games of the 1972 season. He had to rest up for the play-offs. The Pirates were in first place in the National League East and would once again be facing the Cincinnati Reds.

The play-off series opened in Pittsburgh. The pitching of Steve Blass helped lead the Pirates to a 5–1 victory in game one. Clemente went 0 for 3 in the second game. The Reds won 5–3. Game three took place in Cincinnati. Clemente hit a double, helping the Pirates to a 3–2 win. Clemente got two hits in four at-bats in the fourth game. One of them was a home run. This game could have clinched the pennant for the Pirates, but no other Pirate was able to get a hit. Pittsburgh lost 7–1.

The teams were tied at two games apiece when the deciding game was played October 11 at Riverfront Stadium. The Pirates had a 3–2 lead until Cincinnati catcher Johnny Bench hit a home run in the ninth inning and tied the game. A wild pitch by Pirate Bob Moose allowed the Reds to score the run that won them the game. Cincinnati would go on to the World Series. For the Pirates, the season was over.

Taking on the leadership role that by now was comfortable for him, Clemente told his teammates, "Do not hang your heads. Do not . . . hide from the media. You stay out here and talk to them. Be proud to be a Pirate."[7]

Clemente was frustrated about losing the deciding game to Cincinnati on a wild pitch. He had finished the season batting .312, playing in only 102 games, the lowest of his career. He had also won his twelfth Gold Glove award.

Clemente returned to Puerto Rico for the off-season but decided not to play Winter League ball. His back was bothering him, and he wanted to rest it. He stayed active in other ways. Clemente arranged for a local telephone company to sponsor several baseball clinics in Puerto Rico. More than ten thousand youths would participate.

Clemente was always welcomed as a hero in Puerto Rico.

He also managed a Puerto Rican baseball team that played in the Amateur Baseball World Series in Nicaragua. He spent nearly a month in Nicaragua and made many friends there. Clemente left Nicaragua in December and returned to Puerto Rico. On December 23, he learned that an earthquake in Managua, Nicaragua, had killed more than 7,000 people and left more than 250,000 people without homes. The city had no water or electricity. Clemente quickly decided he must do something to help the people.

He immediately took charge of a committee to collect supplies for the earthquake victims. He appeared on Puerto Rican television and radio, asking the citizens of his country to donate supplies. Clemente worked fourteen hours a day through Christmas, gathering food and clothing. He and the committee members were able to raise more than $150,000 for the victims.

Clemente made arrangements for planes to fly the goods to Nicaragua. One of the airplanes was a twenty-year-old, four-engine DC-7. Clemente decided to go on the plane to make sure the goods were being delivered properly. "He had received reports that some of the food and clothing he had sent earlier had fallen into the hands of profiteers," said his friend Cristobal Colon.[8]

Clemente worried that the army in Nicaragua was corrupt and that soldiers were intercepting the supplies. What if the people who needed the supplies were not getting them? Several mechanical breakdowns postponed takeoff, and the plane was dangerously overloaded with supplies. Finally, on December 31, New Year's Eve, the old cargo plane took off from San Juan International Airport about nine o'clock at night. On the plane with Clemente were four other men: Arturo Rivera, who was in charge of the company that owned the plane; Jerry Hill, the pilot; Francisco Matias; the flight engineer; and Rafael Lozano, a friend of Clemente's.

Several people—including Clemente's seven-year-old son, Roberto Jr.—begged Clemente not to make the flight. But Clemente was sure he would be safe. As soon as the plane took off, the pilot realized there was engine trouble. He turned sharply to the left to return to the airport. Suddenly, there were several explosions and the plane nose-dived into the Atlantic Ocean.

Clemente's wife, Vera, received a phone call in the

> **"I don't want anything for myself, but through me I can help lots of people."[9]**
>
> **—Clemente**

early-morning hours. Her husband's plane had gone
down. By dawn of New Year's Day, 1973, many of
Clemente's teammates had heard the news. Rescue
attempts began immediately and continued for eleven
days. Manny Sanguillen, the Pirates' catcher and
Clemente's friend, put on scuba gear and joined a team
of deep-sea divers searching the ocean for any trace of
the passengers. All that was ever found of Clemente was
his briefcase.

**A statue of Roberto Clemente outside Pittsburgh's Three Rivers Stadium
honors the baseball hero and humanitarian.**

Puerto Rico closed down for three days of national mourning for the best-known athlete in the island's history.[10] Radio stations replaced their regular programming with quiet, serious music. A memorial service was held on January 4 at the San Fernando Catholic Church in Carolina, Puerto Rico. Many Pirates came to share their grief, including managers Bill Virdon, Danny Murtaugh, and Harry Walker. Pitcher Steve Blass read a poem.

Baseball commissioner Bowie Kuhn called Clemente "a unique man," adding that "his marvelous playing skills rank him among the truly elite. And what a wonderfully good man he was. Always concerned about others. He had about him a touch of royalty."[11]

Pirates' outfielder Willie Stargell said tearfully, "Pittsburgh lost a heck of a man."[12]

The board of directors for the Baseball Hall of Fame in Cooperstown, New York, decided to bypass the usual rules for voting a player into the hall. Usually, five years had to pass before a player could be voted in. Only once had this rule been broken: Lou Gehrig was admitted to the Hall of Fame when he retired from baseball in 1939.

Clemente was voted in on March 20, 1973, receiving 393 of 424 votes by the Baseball Writers Association. On August 6, he was inducted into the Baseball Hall of Fame. He was the first Latino player to receive this honor. Clemente's eighteen-year career included twelve Gold Gloves, four batting titles, three thousand hits, and a lifetime batting average of .317.

Clemente was considered a national hero and is remembered for his accomplishments off the field as well as on. "Roberto died trying to help people, and he did that often," said Vera Clemente. "We would go on vacation and he would insist on getting away from the tourist areas so that he could talk to the common people about their hopes and dreams."[13]

> "Clemente was a superb professional athlete and a true humanitarian."[14]
>
> —George W. Bush

In July 2003, President George W. Bush awarded Clemente the Presidential Medal of Freedom. This is the highest honor given to a citizen of the United States. The medal was accepted by Clemente's wife, Vera.[15]

Roberto Clemente died as a volunteer trying to help people in their time of need. "He should be a hero to young people," said former major league pitcher Nelson Briles. "There was a great depth to him. He cared deeply about people."[16] Clemente will be remembered, not only as an outstanding athlete, but as someone who tried to make a difference. As Clemente himself once said: "Accomplishment is something you cannot buy. If you have a chance to do something for somebody, and do not make the most of it, you are wasting your time on this earth."[17]

Chronology

1934—Roberto Clemente is born in Carolina, Puerto Rico, on August 18.

1952—Signs first professional contract, with the Santurce Crabbers.

1954—Signs first major league contract, with the Dodgers; is drafted by the Pittsburgh Pirates.

1958—Begins six months of service at Marine Corps boot camp.

1960—Pirates beat Yankees to win World Series; Clemente wins the first of his twelve Gold Glove awards.

1961—Is top All-Star choice for National League right fielder; wins first batting title, becoming first Puerto Rican ever to do so.

1964—Wins second batting title; marries Vera Zabala on November 14.

1965—Wins third batting title.

1966—Reaches 2,000 hits on September 2; wins Most Valuable Player for National League.

1967—Wins fourth and final batting championship.

1970—Roberto Clemente Night is held at Three Rivers Stadium on July 24.

1971—Pirates win World Series against Orioles; Clemente is voted Most Valuable Player of the series.

1972—Gets 3,000th hit; wins twelfth Gold Glove award; dies in plane crash on New Year's Eve on his way to deliver supplies to earthquake victims in Nicaragua.

Chapter Notes

CHAPTER 1. THE DREAM

1. Phil Musick, *Who was Roberto? A Biography of Roberto Clemente* (Garden City, N.Y.: Doubleday & Company, 1974), p. 59.
2. Kal Wagenheim, *Clemente!* (New York: Praeger Publishers, 1973), p. 32.
3. Bruce Markusen, *Roberto Clemente: The Great One* (Champaign, Ill.: Sports Publishing, Inc., 1998), p. 15.
4. Musick, p. 76.

CHAPTER 2. GROWING UP

1. Phil Musick, *Who was Roberto? A Biography of Roberto Clemente* (Garden City, N.Y.: Doubleday & Company, 1974), p. 59.
2. Ibid., p. 52.
3. Ibid., p. 58.
4. Kal Wagenheim, *Clemente!* (New York: Praeger Publishers, 1973), p. 16.
5. Ibid., p. 20.
6. "Latino Legends in Sports," <http://www.latinosportslegends.com> (January 18, 2004).
7. Musick, p. 54.
8. "Latino Legends in Sports" website.
9. Musick, p. 62.
10. Wagenheim, p. 24.
11. Ibid., p. 31.

CHAPTER 3. THE MINOR LEAGUES

1. Phil Dixon with Patrick J. Hannigan, *The Negro Baseball Leagues: A Photographic History* (Mattituck, N.Y.: Amereon House, 1992), p. 26.
2. Tim Kurkjian, *America's Game* (New York: Crown Publishers, Inc., 2000), p. 23.
3. Mark Ribowsky, *A Complete History of the Negro Leagues: 1884 to 1955* (Secaucus, N.J.: Carol Publishing Group, 1995), p. 280.
4. Kurkjian, pp. 22–23.
5. Kal Wagenheim, *Clemente!* (New York: Praeger Publishers, 1973), p. 26.
6. Ibid.
7. Bruce Markusen, *Roberto Clemente: The Great One* (Champaign, Ill.: Sports Publishing Inc., 1998), p. 14.
8. Ibid., pp. 20–21.
9. Ibid., p. 25.

CHAPTER 4. THE PIRATES

1. Kal Wagenheim, *Clemente!* (New York: Praeger Publishers, 1973), p. 42.
2. Bruce Markusen, *Roberto Clemente: The Great One* (Champaign, Ill.: Sports Publishing Inc., 1998), p. 39.
3. Phil Musick, *Who was Roberto? A Biography of Roberto Clemente* (Garden City, N.Y.: Doubleday & Company, 1974), p. 97.
4. "Ballparks: Fields of Dreams," <http://www.baseball-almanac.com/stadium/st_forbes.shtml> (January 18, 2004).
5. Musick, p. 101.
6. Wagenheim, p. 53.
7. Author interview with Nelson Briles, VP, corporate projects for the Pirates, August 25, 2003.
8. Wagenheim, p. 87.

9. Musick, p. 104.
10. Markusen, p. 52.
11. Musick, p. 111.
12. Ibid.
13. Markusen, p. 47.
14. Ibid., p. 48.
15. Ibid., p. 49.
16. Musick, p. 99.

CHAPTER 5. ADJUSTING

1. C.R. Ways, " 'Nobody Does Anything Better Than Me in Baseball,' Says Roberto Clemente," *New York Times*, April 9, 1972, p. SM 38.
2. Bruce Markusen, *Roberto Clemente: The Great One* (Champaign, Ill.: Sports Publishing Inc., 1998), p. 58.
3. Kal Wagenheim, *Clemente!* (New York: Praeger Publishers, 1973), p. 69.
4. Markusen, p. 64.

CHAPTER 6. WORLD CHAMPIONS

1. Bruce Markusen, *Roberto Clemente: The Great One* (Champaign, Ill.: Sports Publishing Inc., 1998), p. 81.
2. Ron Smith, *The Sporting News Selects Baseball's 25 Greatest Moments* (New York: Times Mirror Magazines, Inc., 1999), p. 22.
3. Markusen, p. 81.
4. Ibid., p. 84.
5. Kal Wagenheim, *Clemente!* (New York: Praeger Publishers, 1973), p. 79.
6. Arthur Daley, "Sports of the Times: With Undue Emphasis," *New York Times*, Oct. 13, 1960, p. 45.
7. Smith, pp. 22–23.
8. Ibid., p. 23.
9. Ibid., p. 24.

10. "Bucs Heist Series and the Lid Blows Off," *Life*, October 24, 1960, p. 33.
11. Wagenheim, p. 85.
12. Markusen, p. 104.

CHAPTER 7. ALL-STAR

1. Kal Wagenheim, *Clemente!* (New York: Praeger Publishers, 1973), p. 92.
2. Ibid., p. 131.
3. Author interview with Nelson Briles, VP, corporate projects for the Pirates, August 25, 2003.
4. Musick, p. 165.
5. "Roberto Clemente Quotations by Baseball Almanac," <http://www.baseball-almanac.com/quotes/roberto_clemente_quotes.shtml> (December 3, 2004).
6. Bruce Markusen, *Roberto Clemente: The Great One* (Champaign, Ill.: Sports Publishing Inc., 1998), p. 118.

CHAPTER 8. MOST VALUABLE PLAYER

1. Bruce Markusen, *Roberto Clemente: The Great One* (Champaign, Illinois: Sports Publishing Inc., 1998), p. 141.
2. Kal Wagenheim, *Clemente!* (New York: Praeger Publishers, 1973), p. 131.
3. Phil Musick, *Who was Roberto? A Biography of Roberto Clemente* (Garden City, New York: Doubleday & Company, 1974), p. 211.
4. Wagenheim, p. 141.
5. Musick, p. 215.
6. Ibid.
7. Wagenheim, p.138.
8. Ibid., p. 151.
9. Musick, p. 133.

10. Markusen, p. 157.
11. Wagenheim, p. 147.
12. Markusen, pp. 175–176.
13. Ibid., p. 184.

CHAPTER 9. WORLD CHAMPIONS . . . AGAIN

1. Kal Wagenheim, *Clemente!* (New York: Praeger Publishers, 1973), p. 172.
2. Bruce Markusen, *Roberto Clemente: The Great One* (Champaign, Ill.: Sports Publishing Inc., 1998), p. 195.
3. Ibid.
4. Wagenheim, p. 61.
5. Ibid.
6. Geoffrey C. Ward and Ken Burns, *Baseball: An Illustrated History* (New York: Alfred A. Knopf, 1994), p. 425.
7. Ibid.
8. Wagenheim, p. 145.
9. "El Barrio Mourns Its Community Hero," *New York Times*, January 3, 1973, p. 32.
10. Ibid.
11. Larry Schwartz, "Clemente Quietly Grew in Stature," <http://espn.go.com/classic/biography/s/Clemente_Roberto.html> (December 16, 2004).
12. C.R. Ways, "'Nobody Does Anything Better Than Me in Baseball,' Says Roberto Clemente," *New York Times*, April 9, 1972, p. SM 38.
13. Murray Chass, "Not a Souped-Up Version, Just the Normal Clemente," *New York Times*, October 16, 1971, p. 17.
14. Chass, p. 17.
15. Markusen, p. 278.
16. Wagenheim, p. 205.
17. <http://www.toptown.com/hp/66/roberto.htm> (January 18, 2004).

CHAPTER 10. A LIFETIME OF ACCOMPLISHMENTS

1. Joseph Durso, "Troubles Dog Clemente, Series Hero," *New York Times*, February 23, 1972, p. 47.
2. "Clemente to Be Given Honorary Doctorate," *New York Times*, March 12, 1972, p. S8.
3. Durso, "Troubles Dog Clemente."
4. Murray Chass, "Clemente's Dream: A Utopian Sports City," *New York Times*, October 21, 1971, p. 62.
5. Ibid.
6. Ibid.
7. Bruce Markusen, *Roberto Clemente: The Great One* (Champaign, Illinois: Sports Publishing Inc., 1998), p. 303.
8. "Clemente, Pirates' Star, Dies in Crash of Plane Carrying Aid to Nicarauga," *New York Times*, January 2, 1973, p. 73.
9. Chass, "Clemente's Dream . . ."
10. "Clemente, Pirates' Star, Dies . . ."
11. Sam Goldaper, "Puerto Rico Goes into Mourning," *New York Times*, January 2, 1973, p. 48.
12. Ibid.
13. Ross Newhan, "Clemente's Legacy Is Told in Human Terms," June 3, 2003. <http://www.latimes.com> (January 18, 2004).
14. "Presidential Medal of Freedom Winners," <http://www.medaloffreedom.com/2003RecipientsCitations.htm> (December 3, 2004).
15. "Wooden, Clemente Get Freedom Medals," *Philadelphia Inquirer*, July 24, 2003, p. D2.
16. Author interview with Nelson Briles, VP, corporate projects for the Pirates, August 25, 2003.
17. Newhan, "Clemente's Legacy Is Told . . ."

Further Reading

Books

Engel, Trudie. *We'll Never Forget You, Roberto Clemente*. New York: Scholastic, 1997.

Garcia, Kimberly. *Roberto Clemente*. Bear, Del.: Mitchell Lane Publishers, 2003.

Kingsbury, Robert. *Roberto Clemente*. New York: Rosen Publishing Group, 2003.

Marquez, Heron. *Roberto Clemente: Baseball's Humanitarian Hero*. Minneapolis, Minn.: Carolrhoda Books, 2005.

Walker, Paul Robert. *Pride of Puerto Rico: The Life of Roberto Clemente*. New York: Harcourt, 1991.

Internet Addresses

The Official Roberto Clemente Website
<http://www.robertoclemente21.com>

Roberto Clemente, BaseballLibrary.com.
<http://www.baseballlibrary.com/baseballlibrary/ballplayers/C/Clemente_Roberto.stm>

The Roberto Clemente Page, with photos and links.
<http://www.geocities.com/Colosseum/Field/9877/clemente.html>

Index

Page numbers for photographs are in **boldface** type.